the power of partnership

Principles and Practices for Creating Strategic Relationships Among Nonprofit Groups, For-Profit Organizations, and Government Entities

BY PLEXUS CONSULTING GROUP, LLC

Published Cooperatively by
ASAE & THE CENTER FOR ASSOCIATION LEADERSHIP
and
THE U.S. CHAMBER OF COMMERCE

WASHINGTON, D.C.

WASHINGTON, D.C.

The authors have worked diligently to ensure that all information in this book is accurate as of the time of publication and consistent with standards of good practice in the general management community. As research and practice advance, however, standards may change. For this reason it is recommended that readers evaluate the applicability of any recommendations in light of particular situations and changing standards. This book addresses legal matters, but does not provide or constitute legal advice or opinion. Many of the legal topics in the book related to partnerships are potentially significant to tax exempt organizations and associations, and failure to act consistently with Internal Revenue Service rulings or guidance or other applicable law could result in taxability of revenues, loss of tax exempt status, or other liability. It is strongly recommended that all readers consult their individual professional legal and accounting advisers and take action only upon receipt of such advice.

ASAE & The Center for Association Leadership
1575 I Street, NW
Washington, DC 20005-1103
Phone: (202) 626-2723; (888) 950-2723 outside the metropolitan Washington, DC area
Fax: (202) 220-6439
E-mail: books@asaecenter.org
We connect great ideas and great people to inspire leadership and achievement in the association community.

Cover design by Beth Lower
Interior design by Cimarron Design

This book is available at a special discount when ordered in bulk quantities. For information, contact the ASAE Member Service Center at (202) 371-0940.

A complete catalog of titles is available on the ASAE & The Center for Association Leadership web site at www.asaecenter.org.

ISBN-13: 978-0-88034-294-0
ISBN-10: 0-88034-294-3

Printed in the United States of America.

10 9 8 7 6 5 4 3 2 1

Contents

Acknowledgements

ASAE & The Center for Association Leadership and the U.S. Chamber of Commerce are excited about the release of this collaborative research study. Through our partnership, we were able to develop a resource for our memberships that will provide practical guidance in building and sustaining successful strategic alliances. The framework in this book was built on the continuation of research studies conducted by each organization and the combined collaborative efforts to investigate the characteristics of powerful partnerships. A special thanks to those who have helped us articulate the importance of knowing that more can be achieved in partnership than would otherwise be possible.

Particular thanks are given to the staff and leadership of those organizations that are engaged in the partnerships profiled in this book. Their contributions and time were truly valuable to this study. We also wish to acknowledge a number of other people who contributed to the successful completion of this book:

Cynthia D'Amour, MBA
Jefferson C. Glassie, Esq.
Harris Interactive
Aaron H. Hiller, Esq.
Plexus Consulting Group, LLC
Sandy Sabo
Kristen E. Sitchler, Esq.
Jeffrey S. Tenenbaum, Esq.
Ann Thomas, Esq.
Kevin Whorton

Preface

IN JUNE 2006, the U.S. Chamber of Commerce and ASAE & The Center for Association Leadership announced their partnership to conduct research into the ways that organizations build and sustain successful strategic alliances. Drawing upon our members and other industry stakeholders and using a variety of research methodologies—including surveys, focus groups, in-depth interviews, and case profiling—we sought to identify the determinants and characteristics of powerful partnerships among nonprofit, for-profit, and governmental organizations.

In retrospect, our partnership itself offers a case study. It shows how two organizations, both committed to promoting the competitiveness of the association sector within the wider business community, could join together and leverage their distinct but complementary skills to produce greater results than could be achieved individually.

Built on a long relationship of mutual trust and respect, this partnership between the U.S. Chamber and ASAE & The Center illustrates the process of partnership development that we chose to explore in this research. At the time, each of our organizations was engaged in research related to the competencies of high performing associations. When the two research projects were published—*The Future of the Competitive Association* (U.S. Chamber, 2005) and *7 Measures of Success: What Remarkable Associations Do That Others Don't* (ASAE & The Center, 2006)—we saw some important synergies between our research findings. Our goal during subsequent deliberation was to identify a theme that we could, through research collaboration, develop into a resource to effect positive change in service delivery, revenue generation, and member/customer satisfaction.

Among the seven measures differentiating remarkable associations was their selective participation in strategic "alliances with other organizations—whether nonprofit, for-profit, or government…that proved effective in generating revenue, raising awareness around a key issue, or building their organizational brand." Likewise, the Chamber's *Competitive Association* study, concluded that "effective partnerships with other associations, members, for-profit companies, and nonprofit companies will become increasingly critical to association success." Neither research study delved into the characteristics of these powerful partnerships and how partnerships are identified, built, and sustained to increase the competitive positioning of associations. We saw the opportunity to undertake that effort together.

The U.S. Chamber and ASAE & The Center defined a common vision of success and a formula for equal sharing of risk and reward. Expected outcomes, roles, and responsibilities were defined up-front. The resulting book, *The Power of Partnership*, draws on the findings of the study, as well as on observations about real-world partnerships. It explores partnerships as a key strategic capacity builder for leaders and organizations committed to implementing their strategic vision even when their operational and capital resources are less than what is required.

Competitive, goal-driven, remarkable organizations achieve more in partnership with one or more organizations than would otherwise be possible. We hope that *The Power of Partnership* will provide the stimulus and knowledge to help your organization capitalize on its strengths to realize its goals and aspirations.

Special thanks go to the organizations that participated in the three partnerships profiled in this book and to the volunteer leaders and staff who contributed to the successful completion of this thought-provoking study. We hope that leaders reading this book will find inspiration and requisite knowledge to experiment with their own strategic partnerships.

John H. Graham IV, CAE
President & CEO
ASAE & The Center for
Association Leadership

Thomas J. Donohue
President & CEO
U.S. Chamber of Commerce

Introduction

WOULD YOUR ORGANIZATION like to promote government-funded research in its area of focus? Might your business benefit from owning a stake in an association trade show with a track record of growth? Or would you like a government agency's assistance in educating the potential customers of your organization's membership? This book will demonstrate how you can achieve all this—and even more—thanks to partnering.

Partnerships enable organizations to achieve critical goals that they could not otherwise reach on their own, whether from a lack of financial resources, staffing, time, expertise, credibility, or connections. When organizations have the will to pursue a goal, partnerships just might provide the way.

In fact, partnerships have the flexibility to adapt to most any situation or circumstance, making them ideally suited to meeting today's fast-paced management challenges and opportunities. Partnering allows organizations to achieve what they could not otherwise have done on their own—in other words, this management technique extends what is possible for an organization to achieve without having to borrow, seek grants, merge, or be acquired by a larger entity.

But partnering is a tough concept to tackle, in part because the term itself is so broadly used in numerous and imprecise ways. In common language, for example, any good relationship is typically referred to as a "good partnership"—even if it is not a partnership in the strict, legal definition of the term.

For the purposes of this study, a partnership is defined as a cooperative agreement between two or more organizations where involved parties share the profits and/or losses of the activities they undertake. The term *partnership,* therefore, implies that both parties can benefit if the relationship

Primary Benefits of Partnering

Through the focus groups, questionnaires, and in-depth interviews that formed this study, the following emerged as the five main reasons that nonprofit organizations enter into partnerships.

1. **Share resources.** Not having to go it alone means the partners can achieve more together—and possibly at less cost—than they could afford to do on their own. Furthermore, because each one's resources are specialized—tailored to the markets each serves—the partners can apply their individual "inside knowledge" to achieving the same goal and possibly achieve better results than outsiders trying to do the same.

2. **Reach broader market segments.** Nonprofit executives say a partnership succeeds when it serves the organization's community, for example, by providing a product or service that meets members' needs. In effect, partnerships should enrich the experience of customers and members that each partner serves, while also expanding each partner's reach into new or broader market segments.

3. **Advance the organization's mission.** Whether the goal is strengthening member education programs, lobbying for legislative solutions to business issues, or increasing public awareness, partnerships can support an organization's reason for being. Once a nonprofit has had a successful partnering experience, it typically seeks other organizations with which to collaborate on mission-oriented activities.

4. **Develop new ways of working.** Partnerships enable organizations to expand their educational experience, especially when the other parties are from a different sector and thus bring a different mindset. Well-functioning partnerships serve as a private tutorial for learning new ways of doing business and provide different perspectives on familiar issues.

5. **Gain access to additional resources.** Partnering provides access to networks and contacts that may not otherwise be available or even known to the partners individually. Through partnerships, for example, nonprofits might be able to attract high-profile conference speakers or greater attention from influential policymakers. Similarly, for-profits might gain additional credibility and a wider market for their products and services.

succeeds—and both partners may lose something should the arrangement fail in some way. They share the risks equally.

Further, this book looks at strategic partnerships. "Strategic" implies an action or approach that furthers the long-term mission of an organization. In other words, these partnerships are not conceived simply as tactical solutions to short-term needs. Rather, they are pivotal relationships that help each organization realize its mission better, faster, more efficiently, or more profitably than it could otherwise do on its own.

To be sure, developing such pivotal relationships opens a new world of possibilities and opportunities. But that world, which comes with organizational, legal, and human complexities of its own, can be tricky to navigate. *The Power of Partnership* will help you chart the appropriate course for your organization and its particular goals.

Four Stages

This book, itself the product of a partnership between the U.S. Chamber of Commerce and ASAE & The Center for Association Leadership, is written for executives involved in the management of nonprofit organizations as well as for-profit businesses. Its goal is to help you understand the principles and practices underlying powerful partnerships so that you can employ partnering as a strategic management tool.

Chapter 1 identifies and distinguishes the essential elements of partnerships, as well as other critical characteristics and considerations that contribute to productive and successful relationships of this kind. The next four chapters will guide you through these four stages:

Readiness—Preparing your organization to partner (Chapter 2).

Identification—Finding the right partner, at the right time (Chapter 3).

Formation—Formalizing the partnership (Chapter 4).

Maintenance—Managing the relationship (Chapter 5).

For a reality check, you'll also find information about what a partnership is *not*, as well as a discussion, in Chapter 6, of failed partnerships—including signs of trouble and strategies for a graceful departure. And, at the end of each chapter, a list of talking points appears. These "conversation starters" offer one means of applying the information to your own situation by engaging others in discussions about partnership possibilities.

Appendix A delves into the legal considerations of working with another organization. In it, Jeffrey S. Tenenbaum, Esq., and colleagues from Venable

LLP discuss basic terminology and explain the tax and intellectual property implications involved in forming partnerships. Appendix B offers several sample documents, including a simple Memorandum of Understanding as well as a detailed contract. Although these samples in no way substitute for the advice of your legal counsel, they provide a glimpse at the legal underpinnings of various types of partnerships.

What might prove especially helpful are the three profiles in partnering, all of which involve at least one membership organization. The profiles, undertaken as part of the research, are presented in Chapter 1 but also referred to throughout the text. They provide a "real world" perspective by taking you behind the scenes of three successful partnerships for a glimpse at the contracts, compromises, and commitments required.

To protect the confidentiality of the organizations that so willingly shared the details of their arrangements, challenges, and results, each of these partnerships is referred to throughout the text by a generic name: Health Coalition, Joint Educational Conference, and Trade Show LLC.

A Four-Pronged Approach

The book's content is based upon an examination of partnerships between and among nonprofit organizations in several sectors—including trade associations, professional societies, and philanthropic organizations—and for-profit companies and governmental entities. The intent was to uncover similarities as well as differences in the way partnering was conceived and managed in different types of organizations and sectors.

The research, conducted in 2006 and 2007, had four facets:

- **Virtual focus groups.** Conducted by Harris Interactive, the three Advanced Strategy Labs used polling and open-ended questions to gather opinions and observations from association executives and consultants and vendors to the association sector. Participants were asked what forces drive associations to seek partnerships, what challenges are often faced, and which attributes describe successful strategic partnerships.
- **Exploratory questionnaire.** Findings from the virtual focus groups formed the basis for a detailed questionnaire that garnered responses from equal percentages of trade association and professional society executives. Questions focused on why partnerships succeed or fail and what prompts associations to partner with for-profit businesses, government agencies, and other nonprofits.

- **In-depth interviews.** The findings from the questionnaire were used to identify organizations that are currently engaged in partnerships or have been in the past. Harris Interactive then conducted in-depth interviews with representatives of seven partnerships, exploring such questions as "What were the initial expectations of the partnership?" and "What measures do you use to gauge the success of the partnership?"
- **Profiles of partnerships.** Plexus Consulting Group, LLC, in combination with ASAE & The Center for Association Leadership, identified three partnerships to profile, based on participation in the previous research, the type of partnership, and the reason for the partnership. The resulting analysis identifies how different organizations respond to various aspects of developing and maintaining partnerships.

Throughout the process, extensive secondary research was completed around the topic of partnership to provide background and support the findings of this study. Results of the literature search have been incorporated into the "References and Additional Resources" section.

Going for the Goal

Other than involving at least one membership organization, the partnerships studied as part of this research bore little resemblance to one another. One, for example, had a goal of generating greater revenue, while another had an education-related goal and operated on the assumption that the partnership's efforts would lose money. One partnership came together quickly on the strength of a handshake; another involved more than a year of negotiations and numerous meetings with attorneys.

As different as their goals and formation, however, the partnerships share some success factors. Summarized in Chapter 7, these approaches, tips, and techniques may prove helpful when your organization or business takes its next step toward partnering. Anyone who reads this book will come away with an appreciation for the use and value of partnering as a strategic tool for growth and for fulfilling an organization's mission.

chapter one

Essentials of Partnering

THE WORD **PARTNERSHIP** typically generates a warm, friendly feeling. It conjures up the image of people united in a common cause or activity, striving to work together to accomplish something each would have difficulty doing on its own.

Here's the sobering truth: One of every two partnerships fail. That's according to "When to Ally and When to Acquire," a study of more than 1,000 partnerships reported in *Harvard Business Review* (July/August 2004). Clearly, given that success rate of 50 percent, partnering either doesn't come naturally to many organizations or its requirements produce more pain than gain.

But when organizations make a commitment to partnering and the compromises it entails, they can achieve far more than would be possible on their own. Working with others may enable your organization to stretch resources even further, reach new markets ripe for expansion, or undertake a strategic initiative that would otherwise be too much of a strain or a drain on personnel and finances.

Basic Working Relationships

Organizations can work together in many different ways, through client-vendor relationships and sponsorships to name just two. More complex working relationships include partnerships, mergers, and acquisitions.

Coming to Terms

Partnership—A cooperative agreement between two or more organizations where, without subsuming their individual identities, the involved parties share the profits and/or losses of the activities they undertake together.

Merger—Two or more organizations legally join together to become a single entity, without eclipsing any one organization's identity.

Acquisition—One organization takes over, or absorbs, another organization to the point where the acquired organization ceases to exist as an independent entity.

Partnerships—the easiest of these three relationships to enter into—can be based on something as simple as a handshake. They can be identified, formed, and even brought to their natural conclusion in the amount of time needed to negotiate the legalities of most mergers or acquisitions. Because partnerships sometimes lead to mergers and acquisitions, it is important to understand the similarities and differences of the three.

Partnership: In general, a partnership is a cooperative agreement between two or more organizations where, without subsuming their identities, involved parties share the profits and/or losses of the activities they undertake. Additionally—and more important—partners share the risks as well as the rewards generated by their partnership. Partnerships can produce benefits such as financial gain, program content enrichment, and market expansion, but they can also result in liabilities to their members, both collectively and as individuals.

Consequently, the possibility of failure for all parties in a partnership comes with the desire for success. There is no greater incentive for success than both partners knowing they have something to lose as well as something to gain in their relationship.

Joint ventures represent one type partnership. They are typically built around business segments, issues, products, or events. Particularly useful for partnerships with long-term potential, joint ventures provide a means of defining and managing a partnership through the establishment of a separate legal entity. The principal advantage is that joint ventures give partners a legal shield should a liability concern arise, particularly if there is a need

continued on page 6

Trade Show LLC

Compromising on Control

Partnership: **Trade Show LLC**

Partners: 1 international trade association
1 for-profit publishing company

Goal: Have the largest and most successful trade show in the marketplace

Keys to Success

- Patience to work through complicated business negotiations, detailed legal agreements, and board approval.
- Sharing the same values and desire to build a partnership based on trust and integrity.
- Sharing the same vision for what the event could become and how it would serve the needs of the industry.

Like many membership organizations, an international trade association organized an annual trade show in conjunction with an educational conference. Thanks to a more entrepreneurial approach adopted during the 1990s, the trade show portion of the event had nearly doubled in size. At the same time, despite stepped-up marketing efforts, the conference attendance had leveled off. Increasingly, exhibitors at the trade show—the association's second-largest revenue source—had less traffic at their booths.

When its number of exhibitors also began to diminish, the association approached a for-profit trade show in a niche area of the industry. Empowered by its board of directors to seek out strategic alliances and partnerships, the association made its pitch: Let's team up to increase value and attendance at both of our shows, through co-marketing and co-location.

The for-profit show agreed but ultimately had a different goal than the association did. After stumbling along for two years, with the co-located shows creating more competition than synergy between the organizations, the joint efforts ceased. The association continued its search for ways to improve and expand its trade show.

Negotiations Commence

Not long thereafter, a for-profit publishing company offered to purchase the association's trade show. The company had retired its own show years earlier but wanted to reenter the trade show arena, not only as a means of generating profits and building its brand but also to provide its magazine advertisers with additional exposure to potential customers.

continued on next page

For years, the two organizations had maintained a cordial relationship. Association members subscribed and often contributed to the publishing company's magazine, which, in turn, paid membership dues to the association. Even so, the association had no desire to sell its show outright. Instead, it made a counteroffer to sell a percentage of the show to the publishing company and become partners.

Initially, the for-profit had reservations about sharing ownership and, consequently, control. For example, the publisher wondered whether the association would agree to the changes necessary to make the trade show more appealing to a wider audience. The for-profit wanted to own a majority stake—at least 51 percent—in a joint show.

That proposal met with resistance from the association, which itself wanted 51 percent ownership. Giving up control, some association leaders believed, would lead to the show losing its identification with the association and being perceived solely as the magazine's event. In addition, the association saw a risk in pumping up the trade show's profits for the benefit of the publisher without a corresponding improvement in the educational conference that accompanied the show. Eventually, another counteroffer came from the association, making the case for a 50/50 split in responsibilities and revenues.

Negotiations Continue

Once the for-profit agreed to a 50/50 partnership, both parties called their lawyers. Then, after signing an agreement to never divulge what each organization learned about the other's finances and business practices, they hammered out the details of a formal operating agreement. Ultimately, the partners agreed to the following:

- Establish the trade show as a limited liability corporation (LLC) equally owned by both organizations. The LLC collects all revenues and pays all expenses related to the trade show, then splits the net profits evenly between the two owners.
- Retain the association's name for the trade show.
- Establish a six-member board of directors for the LLC, with each partner appointing three directors.
- Always designate one of the association's representatives as the board chair. With this structure in place, the association demonstrates its majority stake to the IRS and therefore doesn't jeopardize its 501(c)(6) tax-exempt status. In addition, if all three association representatives agree, they can veto any particular action or decision that would conflict with or be contrary to the association's tax-exempt purpose.

- Appoint a nine-member planning committee having four representatives from the for-profit and five from the association. The committee members—typically staff members of the association and the for-profit—have tactical responsibilities primarily related to show management, including the selection of outside vendors; this frees the board to focus on strategic decision making.
- Give the association responsibility for all operational functions related to the trade show. Association staff who work on the show must track their time so that the LLC can provide an appropriate portion of their compensation.
- Give the association overall responsibility for show marketing and database management. The for-profit supports marketing efforts and provides access to its database.
- Evaluate the partnership annually.

Reaching the final partnership agreement required nearly 18 months of back-and-forth discussions. The for-profit accepted the extended timetable the association needed to research implications of the partnership and to garner its governing board's approval.

"I've heard some business executives say they'd never partner with a trade association because of the difficulties involved, but that attitude is just evidence of not having worked with the right groups," observes one of the publishing company's senior staff. "We wanted a fair, balanced partnership built on trust and integrity—and we saw that same set of values on the association's side of the table."

On with the Show

In the first year of the partnership, the trade show increased in size by 20 percent and helped boost attendance for the accompanying educational conference. Evaluations revealed that attendees who had previously attended only part of the trade show now stayed for the entire show as well as the conference. Because many attendees were nonmembers, participating in the partnership gave the association greater visibility within the marketplace and broadened its potential membership pool. From the publishing company's perspective, the trade show not only made a profit but also provided high-quality contacts for magazine advertisers and exhibitors. The two partners have established metrics to use as benchmarks of success for their future trade shows.

The initial success of the trade show partnership prompted the two parties to begin sharing responsibilities for the association's bimonthly magazine. The association, for example, controls and provides the editorial content, while the publishing company sells the advertising and distributes the association

continued on next page

magazine along with its own title (which complements but doesn't compete directly with the association's magazine).

The two also produce webinars together. The association provides the content and speakers, while the for-profit provides the delivery platform. Both market the webinars and share the revenues. With this arrangement in place, participation in webinars has increased by 50 percent.

"You really can't do everything by yourself," says the association's CEO. "Increased competition, among other factors, simply doesn't allow you to go it alone."

continued from page 2

to protect an organization's legal tax status. (For the legal definitions and ramifications of various types of partnerships, please refer to Appendix A.)

Merger: A merger occurs when two or more organizations legally join together to become a single entity. Like partnerships, mergers seek to combine the strengths of the organizations involved without eclipsing any one's identity.

True mergers are "friendly" because the parties involved all agree to take the voluntary action. Still, no merger is easy. The organizations involved must address such potentially contentious issues as which individual aspects to retain, subsume, or eliminate.

The most successful mergers take advantage of a particular market opportunity that can only be achieved through this joining of forces. The least successful mergers tend to involve troubled organizations that come together to ward off individual failure related to shrinking markets, deadly competition, or myriad operational or managerial weaknesses. In such circumstances, mergers tend to have a higher failure rate, perhaps because the problems simply transfer to the new organization.

Although not all partnerships lead to mergers, most mergers begin with partnerships. In "Investigation of Association Mergers," a 2007 study conducted by the William E. Smith Institute for Association Research, the authors point out that partnering is the precursor for all successful mergers between associations.

Acquisition: An acquisition occurs when one organization takes over, or absorbs, another organization. The end result is that the acquired organization ceases to exist as an independent entity. More often than not, a larger organization buys and/or takes over a smaller one. Although this action usually has a negative connotation, it may be friendly.

All sources reviewed for this study agree that two primary drivers motivate takeovers: to increase market share and to increase the array of products and services that an organization can offer. In the for-profit sector, another likely driver is to increase "shareholder value" through "roll-ups" or purchases of similar or complementary organizations; this often enables an organization to gain dominant market share in a particular industry sector or sub-sector.

Acquisitions are sometimes labeled as "mergers" to avoid alienating the customers or shareholders of the acquired organization. Typically, the camouflage fools no one unless the acquired organization's products, services, and operational structure are left in place. The acquired entity is less likely to lose its identity when it has a name brand that can contribute to the acquiring organization's strategy to increase market share or diversify.

The Comfort Factor

Based on responses to the research's exploratory questionnaire, association executives feel most comfortable pursuing partnerships with organizations structured like their own.

Three out of five respondents (60%) say that if they could form only one strategic partnership in the next year, they'd choose to work with another association or nonprofit organization—primarily because they believe two nonprofits are more likely to have shared goals and values. In addition, approximately one in three prefer other nonprofits as partners because vast cultural differences are less likely to exist (36%) and because a for-profit won't have goals that match their association's goals.

If restricted to only one partnership, fewer than one in five respondents would choose to form it with a for-profit company (19%) or a government entity (16%).

Types of Partnerships Involving Nonprofits

Most partnerships fall into two general categories. They can be *task oriented*—designed for a specific purpose or project, such as organizing a conference, producing a publication, or organizing a lobbying effort. Or, they are *process oriented*, in which the value of the partnership is derived from carrying out a process with less tangible results, such as marketing or public education.

Whether forming a task-oriented or a process-oriented partnership, nonprofits have a choice of three types of partners. As illustrated by the three profiles in this chapter, here are the types of partnerships in which trade associations, professional societies, and other nonprofit organizations can participate.

Nonprofits with for-profit companies. For-profit companies frequently eye nonprofit organizations as potential partners. In fact, one out of four association executives who participated in the virtual focus groups report being approached by for-profit corporations seeking to partner with them. And 73 percent of companies say that partnerships with nonprofits and other socially responsible organizations will be important in the next three years.

Nonprofits often work with for-profit companies in the context of affinity programs or as corporate sponsors. A true partnership takes that transactional relationship to another level, where the two organizations share the risks as well as the rewards of a common activity (see "Compromising on Control" on page 3).

Usually—but not always—for-profit companies are motivated to partner with nonprofits to generate profits. The same, of course, could be said of the nonprofits' motivation. Another motivating factor is public relations and marketing purposes: The nonprofit lends credibility to a program or event sponsored "for a good cause" by a for-profit company. Managed carefully, such partnerships can reap promotional value for both partners.

Similarly, for-profits and nonprofits may partner in the name of social responsibility—being a good corporate citizen. Some of these initiatives may flow from state and federal regulations, such as the Community Re-investment Act (CRA) that requires financial institutions to re-invest in their local communities. But, increasingly, for-profit corporations see that they can do well by doing good, and they recognize a natural fit in partnering with nonprofit organizations that already have access to target audiences, a delivery structure in place, and credibility within the community.

Nonprofits with other nonprofits. Professional societies, especially those having similar memberships, often partner on task-oriented projects such as conferences, government relations efforts, and grassroots lobbying. The partnership enhances each organization's ability to achieve success by mobilizing the full resources of the market or professional sector. Partnerships to jointly produce meetings and conventions, for example, enable nonprofits

Private Interests and the Public Good

The National Council for Public and Private Partnerships (NCPPP), Washington, DC, defines a public-private partnership (PPP) as "a contractual agreement between a public agency (federal, state or local) and a private sector entity. Through this agreement, the skills and assets of each sector (public and private) are shared in delivering a service or facility for the use of the general public. In addition to the sharing of resources, each party shares in the risks and rewards potential in the delivery of the service and/or facility."

According to NCPPP, such partnerships have a greater likelihood of success when these six components are present.

Political Leadership. A successful partnership can result only if there is commitment from "the top." The most senior public officials must be willing to be actively involved in supporting the concept of PPPs and taking a leadership role in the development of each partnership. A well-informed political leader can play a critical role in minimizing misperceptions about the value to the public of an effectively developed partnership. Equally important, there should be a statutory foundation for the implementation of each partnership.

Public Sector Involvement. Once a partnership has been established, the public sector must remain actively involved in the project or program. Ongoing monitoring of the performance of the partnership is important in ensuring its success. This monitoring should be done daily, weekly, monthly, or quarterly for different aspects of each partnership; the frequency is often defined in the business plan and/or contract.

A Well-Thought-Out Plan. Know what you expect of the partnership beforehand. A carefully developed plan (often done with the assistance of an outside expert in this field) will substantially increase the probability of success of the partnership. This plan most often will take the form of an extensive, detailed contract, clearly describing the responsibilities of both the public and private partners. In addition to attempting to foresee areas of respective responsibilities, a good plan or contract will include a clearly defined method of dispute resolution (because not all contingencies can be foreseen).

A Dedicated Income Stream. While the private partner may provide the initial funding for capital improvements, there must be a means of repayment of this investment across the long term of the partnership. The income stream can be generated by a variety and combination of sources (fees, tolls, shadow tolls, tax increment financing, or a wide range of additional options) but must be ensured for the length of the partnership.

continued on next page

Communication with Stakeholders. More people will be affected by a partnership than just the public officials and the private sector partner. Affected employees, the portions of the public receiving the service, the press, appropriate labor unions, and relevant interest groups will all have opinions—and frequently significant misconceptions—about a partnership and its value to all the public. Communicate openly and candidly with these stakeholders to minimize potential resistance to establishing a partnership.

The Right Partner. The "lowest bid" is not always the best choice for selecting a partner. The "best value" in a partner is critical in a long-term relationship. A candidate's experience in the specific area of partnerships being considered is an important factor in identifying the right partner.

Source: National Council for Public and Private Partnerships; www.ncppp.org.

to hedge against the vagaries of attendance—especially if they have a narrowly targeted or niche audience. Joint marketing helps on the revenue side, and joint responsibility to fulfill hotel and facility guarantees softens the risk that each partner must assume.

Nonprofit-to-nonprofit partnerships in process-oriented programs are also common. For example, professional societies often partner with nonprofit foundations, particularly to implement credentialing programs. The foundation sets and measures standards, while the professional society provides the educational and training programs that enable their members and the market to reach the standards. Such synergistic partnerships commonly produce a benefit for the organizations involved, as well as for society at large.

Partnerships among nonprofits are particularly useful when groups serving related professions or industry sectors find common cause on a public policy issue. The unified voice that emerges from combined membership bases can be difficult for lawmakers or regulators to ignore. Nonprofit coalitions can claim, with legitimacy, that they represent more than a narrow segment of the economy and work on behalf of the broader public good (see "The Power of Four" on page 11).

Nonprofits with government agencies. Nonprofits frequently view government agencies or departments as having goals and market bases similar to their own, which gives potential partnerships a solid start. Government agencies may also have the additional funding and resources that nonprofits

continued on page 13

Health Coalition

The Power of Four

Partnership: **Health Coalition**

Partners: 1 professional society
3 voluntary health organizations

Goal: Increase advocacy at the federal level for research funding

Keys to Success

- A tight focus on the coalition's goal, which takes precedence over the goals of individual partners.
- Frequent, purposeful communication.

More than a dozen years ago, three voluntary health organizations and one professional society that worked in the same area of medicine and research came together to form the Health Coalition to enhance their advocacy efforts. Given their specialized areas of focus and limited resources, two of the organizations otherwise had little hope of gaining the attention of legislators and policymakers in Washington, DC. As the executive director of one of the coalition's partners observes, "It is better to pursue congressional initiatives and funding together, as there is greater strength in numbers."

The Health Coalition focuses on advocacy at the federal level, jointly funding a contract with a lobbying firm to represent its interests on Capitol Hill. Its activities include writing reports, preparing testimony, and making joint visits to influential lawmakers and key policymakers. To date, the four organizations—which do not directly compete for members or funding—have not expanded the partnership to include other joint activities, such as producing educational materials and organizing conferences.

An Equal Say

Because the coalition does not generate revenue, its members saw no need to formalize the partnership with a legally binding agreement. Each organization covers its own staffing and overhead costs associated with participating in the coalition. At the same time, each organization is a party to the formal contract with the lobbying firm.

The coalition revisits the contract annually, as part of its strategic planning for the next legislative session, and specifies goals, expectations, and payment schedules. Together, the partners assess the lobbying firm's performance and determine whether to retain it for another year.

continued on next page

When it comes to deciding where the lobbying firm will focus its attention, the democratic process prevails. Each partner has an equal voice in the coalition's activities. What differs is the funding level, with payments to the lobbying firm based on organizational budget. The two largest organizations each provide 45 percent of the contract's total, while the two smallest each fund 5 percent. This enables two of the organizations to gain lobbying representation and the other two to strengthen their voice. The funding differences aren't significant in the partnership; it's more important that each partner has an equal say.

In this way, the smaller organizations can leverage their limited resources to influence policy while the coalition as a whole gains the support of niche markets that draw attention to the overall identified health concern. Each organization brings something unique and necessary to the coalition, and each has an incentive to participate.

Typically, the executive director or CEO of each organization serves as the representative to the coalition. These representatives review a monthly report provided by the lobbying firm and, at a minimum, have quarterly telephone conferences to discuss strategic priorities and initiatives. Thanks to those calls and many emails, says one executive director, "It feels like we are all in the same city."

Once a year, all four executives convene face to face for the coalition's strategic planning meeting. Research scientists from each organization join them in planning the coalition's agenda. Any new initiatives related to the coalition's goal emerge from discussions during these annual sessions, rather than from any pronouncements handed down by the four organizations' governing boards.

Crisis Points

Several times in its history, the Health Coalition has experienced turnover as executive directors and CEOs have changed at the partnering organizations. The consensus is that such changes, while occasionally unsettling, have not affected the coalition's ability to remain focused on its goals.

"Personalities can affect the coalition, but the mission takes precedence," says a staff member from one of the organizations. "They all realize they need to work together and get along in order to get heard by those on the Hill. The overall goals of the group cannot be affected by squabbling."

Whenever other organizations have expressed interest in joining the coalition, the four partners have done their due diligence and concluded that either the other group's mission wasn't a good fit or the timing wasn't right. At one point, another organization's overture prompted the coalition's representatives to focus more on working well together, to show a cohesive, united front to the industry. None has ruled out expanding the coalition in the future.

To date, the Health Coalition's work has generated millions in funding for research and education related to the health concern common to the four partners. None of the four organizations is a recipient of the funding, which is channeled to either health-related government agencies or independent research facilities. The four partners work together for the greater good of the field, rather than for individual gain.

continued from page 10

see as necessary for reaching their objectives. In addition, partnering with a federal or state-level government entity can give a nonprofit's members the opportunity to meet policymakers face to face.

In return, government entities receive quick and direct access to large blocs of key constituent groups who can be identified as well as reached through the nonprofit's existing structure. Because membership organizations tend to represent broad swaths of the economy, as opposed to a single company or investor group, they offer government entities a way to access critical target audiences without any perceived favoritism.

Finally, since the 1990s, the federal government has abided by the policy that taxpayer-funded programs should not compete against or seek to replace similar programs run by the private sector. This is particularly true for job training or retraining, outplacement services, and product and professional standards setting. By seeking public–private partnerships, government agencies recognize the efficiencies of combining efforts to advance and enhance the public good.

The key constraint for both parties is entering into any partnership that has a perceived conflict of interest. In other words, it is highly improbable that government regulatory agencies would want to partner with organizations whose membership they are responsible for regulating. This may well be a problem for those nonprofits whose missions emphasize their lobbying function.

Most associations tend to congregate in and around capital cities to fulfill their function as advocates for a particular profession or industry sector. In this advocacy role, associations have to deal with contentious issues with their legislative or regulatory counterparts. Or, if these relations are not contentious, both sides will usually admit that they eye the other with a certain amount of suspicion. For these reasons, true partnerships between public and private entities are rare but not impossible (see "Built on a Handshake" on the next page).

continued on page 16

Joint Educational Conference

Built on a Handshake

Partnership: **Joint Educational Conference**

Partners: 1 state-level trade association
1 department of state government

Goal: Produce a top-notch educational event for the benefit of local and state officials

Keys to Success

- Structured planning and sharing of responsibilities.
- Revisiting the partnership annually to ensure it meets attendees' changing needs.

A state association had a lot going for it, including high credibility among its members, involvement with policymakers, and extensive information about the state's needs. But it also had an annual business conference, geared toward customers of the association's members, that was experiencing steady declines in attendance.

Interested in reaching a larger and more diverse audience, the association initially considered partnering with other membership organizations related to its members' customer base. The risk of losing ownership in the conference—especially to a somewhat competing organization—always proved an obstacle. More promising was the possibility of working with a state-level department that annually hosted several conferences, one of which overlapped the goals and audience of the association's own conference.

The association's executive director contacted the government agency and asked a simple question: Might it be willing to produce a joint educational conference? More than a decade has passed since the department's director said "yes."

Give and Take

Having concluded they should work together, the two organizations moved forward on the basis of a simple "gentlemen's agreement" that outlined a 50/50 partnership and fully shared responsibilities. "It was easier to say, 'Let's try it' without going to the attorneys first," says a representative of the government entity. "We felt it was worth the risk to partner without the legalities because we could simply discontinue the partnership if it didn't work out."

Neither group called an attorney or felt compelled to draft a multi-page contract to formalize the partnership. Both wanted to devote their time and resources to the partnership itself and believed the presence of lawyers might inhibit discussions and hinder their willingness to compromise. And compromise they did.

For marketing purposes, the association agreed to retire its own conference brand and use the conference name and slogan coined by the government agency. The association also took on a greater share of the financial responsibility; it provides two thirds of the conference budget versus the one third provided by the government entity. For its part, the department of state government provides the personnel needed to organize logistics and staff the one-day conference. It also maintains, updates, and controls the list of participants, which the association can access but not use for its own purposes. After working out each partner's responsibilities, the two groups signed a simple letter of agreement.

Above all, the partners agree that their goal is to produce the best possible educational event for local and state officials interested in promoting economic development in their areas—not to generate revenue. The event is not self-sustaining. Both parties heavily subsidize the conference, which carries a minimal registration fee to encourage greater participation. Although they welcome exhibitors who can supply attendees with relevant solutions and services, the partners rarely sell corporate sponsorships. They wish to keep the conference true to its educational mission and not become sidetracked by the potential for profits.

Sharing the Planning

Planning for the full-day conference—which typically features about 16 educational sessions and two dozen speakers from business, industry, and government—falls to a planning committee with equal representation from both partners.

To jumpstart the planning process, the association surveys the primary audience for the conference to determine their most pressing needs and relevant content. Next, the association prepares a "master worksheet" that the planning committee members use to identify gaps in planned content versus the survey results. They also benchmark the conference against similar conferences held in other states, looking for areas that could be improved. The committee convenes at least three in-person meetings, supplemented by teleconferences, with the workload shared equitably among members.

Throughout the planning process, the committee focuses on one goal: How can we have the best conference? That translates into each partner putting aside any individual notions of how the conference should unfold and remaining open to the other's ideas. "I've been on committees where one side would dig in its heels and not move, but this group has always been willing to

continued on next page

communicate and make decisions based on give-and-take," says the association's CEO.

Minor issues have surfaced only when politics has intervened in the partnership. One year, for example, the government agency was pressured to divert attendees from the conference to the statehouse as a show of support for one of the governor's legislative initiatives—a surprise move that did not play well with some attendees and with the association.

Nor was the association especially pleased about the state's request to sign a formal partnership agreement that specified accountabilities and superseded the longstanding letter of agreement. Based on the length and strength of the partnership, however, the association signed the new agreement. It reviews the partnership contract annually and is prepared to opt out whenever a good fit no longer exists.

Although the two partners have considered inviting other organizations to join them in producing the conference, they have not made any moves in that direction. In its current configuration, the partnership results in a conference that attracts more than 600 people annually, garners excellent evaluations from attendees, and draws the attention of policymakers as well as the media. By joining forces, both groups met their goal—and then some—of reaching a larger audience with high-level education.

continued from page 13

What Partnering is Not

Partners. Partnering. Partnerships. Because people use these words so frequently, their exact meaning loses its power. Certainly, someone described as "partner" has a positive connotation. The term generally refers to someone who is there for another through thick and thin—someone who can be relied on.

In this spirit, nonprofits often use the term *business partners* to describe contracting business entities with whom they have positive relationships. In a commercial, vendor–buyer relationship, money is exchanged for a specific product or service provided. As associations and other types of organizations become familiar with one another's operations and expectations, sponsorships may become an option. With sponsorships, the sponsor provides funding to expand or create a value in the organization's mission, often in exchange for the opportunity to assist with or guide the implementation of that defined value offering.

But are these true partnerships? More often than not, the answer is no. When two organizations enter into a contractual relationship in which one agrees to provide products or services to another for a price—and in which the liability, should something go wrong, is borne by one party alone—then no matter how long-standing or satisfying the relationship, it is not a partnership.

Partnerships, in the truest sense of the word, involve organizations that share equally in the financial risk associated with the product, service, or value offering. This jointly shared risk differentiates partnerships from more purely commercial, transactional relationships. Partners have synergistic, strategic reasons for working together. Each party focuses intently on the success of the relationship because its own success or failure is also at stake. Such is not necessarily the case in vendor and sponsor contracts. Vendors and sponsors reflect more tactical relationships of buyers and sellers of products or services.

As an example, one state association developed a positive, close relationship with a for-profit company it hired to develop a proprietary product. In time, the association came to not only categorize the vendor as a "partner" but also provide office space for several of the company's employees. The association's chief executive officer serves on the company's board of directors, and an employee of the company serves on the association's board.

Yet the contract between the two entities clearly states that the company provides the association with a service for a specified cost and bears no responsibility or liability should problems arise. Moreover, should the association ever fall behind on its payments, the vendor would immediately cease providing services. As mutually beneficial as this relationship is, it is not a partnership; it remains a commercial transaction.

The litmus test of a partnership is the extent to which the parties involved equally bear the rewards of success and the risks of failure. Keeping this distinction clear is critical to understanding partnerships as a strategic management tool. It also may keep association managers from entering into questionable business deals where risk is disproportionately distributed under the delusion that the relationship is a "partnership."

Talking Points

- What might our organization gain from participating in a partnership with an association or nonprofit organization? A for-profit company? A government agency or department?
- Do we currently lack the staffing, resources, or contacts to complete a specific task or process essential to our organization's growth and stability?
- What successful partnerships currently exist within our industry, profession, or sector? Who are the partners? Why do we believe they achieved their goals?

chapter two

Readiness: Preparing to Partner

WHAT DRIVES ORGANIZATIONS to partner? The partnerships researched for this book demonstrate how nonprofit organizations, as well as small- and medium-sized for-profit enterprises, can do more with less. That is, they can achieve greater return on investment—as well as register greater progress toward strategic goals—with little to no investment in overhead expenses.

The vast majority (86%) of the respondents to the exploratory questionnaire say the most important accomplishment of a strategic partnership is "to achieve a goal that the association could not achieve alone." In the nonprofit world of the respondents, most often that goal is to

- Increase membership
- Increase resources
- Increase revenue
- Enhance visibility and/or brand
- Expand current markets (or develop new markets)
- Minimize the risk inherent in any innovation
- Maximize use of resources

In the for-profit world, executives turn to strategic partnerships to expand their businesses and maximize shareholder value. According to a 2008 survey by the Economist Intelligence Unit on behalf of AT&T, 75 percent of respondents plan to increase their use of collaborative relationships. Specifically, these senior executives want to bring greater economies, talent, and efficiencies to their operations. Other business goals commonly articulated by business executives include expanding into new markets, sharing the development or implementation costs of technology, developing new products, and enhancing value or selection for customers.

These examples represent responses to the trends driving change globally—the same trends affecting for-profit as well as nonprofit organizations. For instance, organizations with a high-cost infrastructure and mature or stagnant markets often lose business to more fleet and nimble organizations that employ new technologies, as confirmed by a survey of small and medium-sized enterprises conducted in the 1990s by Deloitte Touche Tohmatsu.

And not only has the pace of change picked up but also the strategic needs of the markets served have changed. The customers and members living in today's "Have it My Way" world expect high quality, competitively priced, and tailor-made products and services—not a one-size-fits-all approach. Smaller, under-capitalized, and under-staffed organizations become able to fulfill those expectations by finding partners that can fill their gaps in knowledge, geography, technology, funding, or personnel.

Partnering is a strategic management tool ideally suited to nonprofits and any businesses that are constantly challenged to narrowly focus on individual needs while providing an array of services. It's also a deliberate strategy for for-profits and nonprofits alike, not a collaboration to enter into lightly.

Each partnership profiled for this study (see Chapter 1) followed the same methodology. First, one of the partners identified a strategic need that it could not achieve on its own (Readiness). Second, the organization engaged its leaders in sorting through a variety of potential partners that might assist in achieving the strategic goal (Identification). Third, an organizational structure was put together that was tailor-made to each partner's strategic needs and operational structures (Formation).

This chapter delves into the first stage of partnership: preparing to partner.

Start with Strategy

Your organization most likely has a strategic plan outlining goals and objectives for the next few years. And some of those strategic goals may represent a "stretch" for the organization in terms of funding or staffing or clout needed to get the job done. Having a well-crafted, mission-focused strategic plan—but not the means to achieve it—can be frustrating, which is where partnering comes in.

Partnering requires a certain humility, a recognition that you can't do it all by yourself. Beyond that, as the ancient Greeks counseled, "Know thyself."

Those early philosophers saw self-awareness as the first step toward acquiring wisdom, advice that holds true for organizations just as for individuals.

For your organization, "Know thyself" translates into ensuring that every stakeholder has a fundamental understanding of the organization's strategic plan. This includes knowing and understanding the following aspects of the organization:

Vision. What does your organization seek to achieve or become in the long term? Your vision should provide succinct focus and meaning to what your organization is all about—both to the outside world as well as to internal stakeholders.

Mission. Your mission states what your organization is in a way that explains how it expects to achieve its vision. Too many organizations have long, wordy mission statements that few people may read. Good mission statements drive your organization. They serve both as motivators and compasses to ensure everyone stays on track.

The ideal mission statement is both inspirational and memorable—it can be recited by every stakeholder in your organization, from your leadership to every constituency served, no matter how small.

Principles. What are the values or principles implied in your mission and reflected in everything your organization does? In other words, what do you stand for? What guidance do you give stakeholders and customers about what is (and is not) permitted? The larger and more widely flung your organization, the more these principles are important.

Goals. What are the measurable strategic goals your organization has set for itself? How have you structured and allocated resources to achieve the objectives that enable the organization to remain faithful to its mission?

Strategic environment. What are your strengths and weaknesses as an organization? These refer to *internal qualities* of your organization, such as organizational culture, finances, the kind and quality of the intellectual property (products and services) offered, and the caliber of staff and volunteer leadership—all things over which you have some degree of control.

Your strategic environment also refers to *external factors* such as the general state of the economy, technological and political developments, and the existence of competing organizations—things that may represent either opportunities or threats to your organization but over which you have no control.

Armed with this knowledge, your stakeholders can articulate the sort of partnerships that would be of most interest. Specifically, a partnership should either build off these strengths to take advantage of opportunities or, alternately, offset or correct strategic weaknesses as well as address threats.

Each of these five key elements should be well-researched and fact-based, reflect the organization's current situation and not be years out-of-date, and represent input from all constituencies. Based on their analysis of these elements, your staff and leaders, as well as stakeholder groups outside your organization, are equipped to know

- What your organization has to offer to potential partners
- Areas in which partnering would be most helpful
- Parameters and considerations around which your organization can (and should) structure partnerships

A Strategic Alignment

Every partnership offers the potential for both gain as well as loss. Money, prestige, and future potential are always at stake. That's why partnerships, although sometimes quite tactical in nature, are always inherently strategic in scope.

"Strategic" implies an action or approach that furthers the long-term strategic mission of an organization. The four organizations that formed the Health Coalition, for instance, came together with the idea of increasing advocacy at the federal level, for the benefit of all their constituencies. Their partnership eventually led to a joint contract with a lobbying organization, but that tactical action was not the stated goal at the outset.

Why is understanding the strategic nature of a partnership so important? Because, based on an analysis of the partnerships researched for this study, they all shared these strategic characteristics:

Complementary missions. Partners "complete" one another by supplying a need or offsetting a deficiency. Partnership is not a zero-sum game in which one partner's gain represents a loss for the other. Rather, the accomplishment of one partner's mission enhances or advances the accomplishment of the other's mission.

Having missions that were in sync enabled the Health Coalition to come together despite differences in size and budget among its four members. It has also enabled them to iron out tactical differences of opinion—and to turn away other organizations that might wish to join the coalition but have missions that are not in line with the four partners'.

WORDS OF ADVICE

"Look for the commonalities of the organizations. Don't try to achieve too much that isn't possible."

– Senior executive, charitable foundation

Compatible goals and interests. If one partner aims to increase value for its members or customers while the other only wants to increase profits, problems will undoubtedly ensue. A partnership between organizations whose goals aren't in sync risks siphoning off precious time and human and financial resources that could be put to better use elsewhere.

The Joint Educational Conference came about because the trade association and government agency found common ground in providing an educational experience for their similar (and slightly overlapping) constituencies. Both focus on the partnership's educational goal, not its financial possibilities. In fact, both partners view the conference as being revenue-neutral, at the best.

As another example of compatibility, both the association and the publishing company involved in the Trade Show LLC had a general interest in partnering before they joined forces. The association's board had approved a strategic plan that included goals for entering into partnerships, and the publishing company had made partnering with trade associations an element of its business model.

Agreement on principles. Remember what your mother told you—birds of a feather flock together! Your partners represent you, whether you intend it or not. So, it is critical their values and operating principles correspond to yours.

The trade association involved in the Trade Show LLC learned this lesson in an earlier attempt at a partnership with a different for-profit company. Operating on principles of trust and integrity, the association agreed to co-locate its conference and trade show with the company's conference and show—only to discover its "partner" was approaching the association's exhibitors independently and offering them "a better deal."

In retrospect, says a senior staff person at the association, during the negotiation period the company "wouldn't share all of the financials and attendance data we needed. We tried to make it work for some time, even though they would agree to something and turn around and do the opposite." When it entered into the Trade Show LLC partnership, the association ensured it did not compromise its principles again.

Strong individual contributions. Each organization brings a vital strength that contributes to the overall vitality of the partnership. In the case of the Joint Educational Conference, the association contributes two thirds of the event budget; although the government agency provides fewer financial resources, its staff handle all of the conference logistics.

Clear understanding of liability. Because they share the risk, partners are "in it together" for good or bad. This produces a sense of commitment to one another and to the partnership in general.

WORDS OF ADVICE

"Partners should be partners through the good and the bad."

– Senior executive, trade association

In the case of the Trade Show LLC, the trade association operated on the assumption that the new partnered show would not produce significant revenue increases for several years. Consequently, its board of directors put some of the profits from the partnership's first effort into the association's reserves, to provide a financial cushion for future years.

Moving Ahead

In addition to the strategic characteristics they shared, the partnerships studied had two other points of common ground.

First, the partners are fully prepared to walk away from a partnership that has ceased serving its function. Even though some of these partnerships have lasted a decade or more, the parties involved take a practical view and revisit their joint efforts—and the results—each year. The partnerships do not endure because of organizational inertia or confusion about goals. Instead, the partnerships are purposeful and considered to be only as valuable or as durable as what they produce.

Second, the organizations studied made a commitment to employing partnering as a strategy for organizational management and growth. Their cultures accommodate the potential rewards as well as the risks a partnership may bring. Even failure—such as the betrayal of trust once experienced by the trade association involved in the Trade Show LLC—does not discourage or dissuade them from continuing down the path to partnership with other organizations.

Being prepared—financially, culturally, and operationally—enabled the partnerships profiled to accomplish the following:

- Gain market intelligence through sharing of resources and information.
- Improve organizational efficiency by accomplishing more with the same amount of resources.
- Increase financial stability by combining financial resources.
- Present a unified view on a particular policy issue.
- Enhance community image through additional media attention and a demonstrated commitment to industry and the membership.
- Increase power and prestige of the partnering organizations.
- Reduce competitive fundraising through the combining of contacts.

These are not insignificant advantages—in fact, they could mean the difference between an organization's growth and stagnation.

Talking Points

- What does our organization seek to achieve in the long term?
- How do we plan to achieve the vision?
- How do we, as an organization, reflect our values and principles?
- What are our organization's strengths and weaknesses?
- In which specific areas might our organization benefit from developing strategic partnerships?
- What could we bring to a partnership?
- What could we hope to gain—and how would that help advance our mission, purposes, and goals?
- Do we need to adapt any business plans or obtain approvals before pursuing potential partnerships?
- Are we prepared to commit the resources needed to form a partnership that may not succeed initially or ever?

chapter three

Identification: Finding the Right Partner

THE FIRST STAGE of partnering requires you to develop a sound self-understanding of your organization's strategic needs. During the second stage (Identification), you initiate the search for the partner(s) that not only fits with your strategic needs but also is open itself to the idea of partnering. Or, sometimes, an opportunity presents itself simply because the organization has completed its preparations and therefore knows what it wants from a partnership.

One association executive tells the story of meeting a representative of a for-profit company at an industry event. The two chatted, and both concluded that their organizations "fit" and "there should be some way for them to work together." Although the executive was not actively searching for a partner, the encounter eventually led to a formal relationship between the two organizations.

This opportunity for a partnership would not have happened had the association executive not been prepared and kept an eye open for potential partners in networking situations. In this instance, both partners had long and prestigious track records in the industry. Leaders of both organizations had known one another for many years, so bonds of trust had had time to develop. Sometimes the best partners are sitting right in front of you.

Opportunity Favors the Prepared

While partnerships are frequently easier to form among and between people and organizations of longstanding acquaintance, such familiarity is not necessarily a prerequisite for a successful partnership. Partnering opportunities abound for virtually every organization everywhere and at any time. But you need to know how and where to look.

Here's a process for identifying and approaching prospective partners.

Decide to be proactive. As part of the Readiness stage, you've already identified areas in your strategic plan where you lack the resources needed to achieve your objectives. Now get more specific within those areas, considering such factors as your organization's political clout, market access, credibility, critical mass of buyers or political constituents, and intellectual property (products and services) that your market needs.

The areas of greatest need will become obvious as you develop the business plans to implement strategy. When you have "hit a wall" in what your organization can accomplish on its own for a particular initiative, try the following steps rather than admit defeat:

- Invite your most well-connected stakeholders to join you in brainstorming ways by which to overcome these obstacles through partnerships. Every organization has multiple "sensors" by which it can obtain critical market information. These sensors can be in the form of staff or volunteer leaders or members at large (in a membership organization).
- For each obstacle, compile a list of possible partners. Include all organizations that operate within your industry, profession, or area—for-profits, other nonprofits, and government entities (international/multinational, federal, state, and local).
- Research the visions, missions, and strategic priorities of these other organizations; identify those that most closely align with or complement your own.
- Ask the group of stakeholders to identify those organizations with which they may have established contacts.
- Drawing on the brainstorming group's experience and connections, identify the strategies and tactics most likely to lead to success in approaching the various potential partners.

Start networking. In the 1990s, when Deloitte Touche Tohmatsu surveyed small- and medium-sized enterprises about partnering, it discovered that these businesses typically found their partners through chambers of commerce and business or professional associations. In other words, they relied on their networks.

Networking is a mindset, part of a purposeful way of conducting your professional life or organizing your business operations. The president of the publishing company that participates in the Trade Show LLC, for example, has built partnering into his business strategy. He actively looks for opportunities to create partnerships and works to establish business relationships with potential partners.

Networking does not come naturally to most people. Those who seem to be born "networkers" are prolific in identifying new clients, members, or business partners. They help their organizations grow and flourish. Some organizations realize this and deliberately foster and encourage a culture in which networking skills are honed and encouraged on the part of their staff and volunteer leadership. To do the same:

- Regularly monitor and attend (if possible) the activities of other organizations (including other nonprofits as well as for-profit and government entities) in your sector or related sectors.
- Systematically seek out and create opportunities for cross-fertilization of ideas among volunteer leaders and staff with these other organizations.
- Have a system in place for capturing data and interpreting market trends beyond your own organization.
- Train staff and volunteer leaders in networking techniques. These sessions should emphasize the importance of adopting a listening, questioning attitude to discern the motivating interests and concerns behind someone's conversation or stories. Effective networking also calls for a solid understanding of the capacities and limits of one's own organization, so you are able to identify how those needs might be satisfied by what the prospective partner has to offer.

WORDS OF ADVICE

"Never enter into a partnership lightly. Know who you are dealing with—know their ethics, their capabilities, and their professionalism."

– Senior executive, trade association

Do your homework. Develop a list of questions to answer about any potential partner, including its mission, demonstrated values, obvious assets, and possible liabilities. Discovering and acknowledging the differences that exist between your organizations will help you anticipate—and prepare to resolve—the conflicts most likely to arise. Most of the partnerships studied involved organizations and leaders that were familiar with one another's work, market segment, credibility, reputation, and so forth. When such mutual familiarity exists, the answers to most "due diligence" questions should be readily found.

Ready, Set, Partner?

Use this list of 10 questions to ascertain your organization's openness and readiness to forge a partnership:

- What is the potential partner's mission? Is it complementary to or compatible with our mission?
- What is the partner's position in the market—is the organization respected and growing or troubled and in decline?
- What assets or hidden liabilities might the partner bring to the table?
- Does the proposed partnership help us achieve a worthy goal that we could not otherwise achieve on our own, with our current resources?
- Are there other potential partners who could do the same thing(s) better?
- Is there a compatibility of organizational cultures as well as the personalities and management styles of the respective decision makers?
- What are the consequences should the partnership fail?
- If the partnership should succeed, what is its future potential?
- Do our senior staff and leaders agree on going forward with this action?
- Do we have the time, means, and interest to invest in managing this relationship?

Your answers to these questions will help determine how (and whether) to proceed with a potential partner and how to structure the relationship. They also may identify areas you must strengthen—or issues you must address—before further pursuing a partnership.

On occasion, however—particularly if your organization is entering a new market—the players are not readily recognizable. Always take great care to do in-depth research and become familiar with the culture, language, and business practices of a potential partner.

- Using reliable primary sources (publicly available materials) and secondary sources (contacts with individuals within your own organization), find out about the people and the organization you intend to deal with. Who are they? What are their needs? How do they make decisions? Is the organizational culture open to or averse to risk? What is the best way for you to present the partnership concept? What questions are they likely to have?
- If you don't have the time to do the research yourself, delegate it to someone within your organization and provide ample resources. Another option is to hire a consultant with experience in partnerships and negotiations. Although you may be the person authorized to sign the final deal, don't engage yourself upfront if you don't have the time to follow through with all of the research required.

Don't assume a reciprocal interest in partnering. The partnership potential that seems obvious to your organization won't necessarily be recognized by the one you approach. Remember the 80-20 rule of the Pareto Principle: Of your overtures to prospective partners, 80 percent may not be fruitful, while 20 percent may succeed.

Although not every contact will result in immediate success, a positive, professional approach often can leave an impression that has positive effects for weeks, months, or even years later. While in the midst of establishing a separate legal entity, for instance, the two partners in the Trade Show LLC approached a third organization they considered "the perfect addition" to the partnership because it represented a large segment of professionals related to the trade show's industry. The two partners produced financial projections and benefits analyses but, ultimately, the potential partner decided against joining in, at least at this time.

"The organization had always functioned in success and thus wasn't ready to take on the risk and see a possible failure," explains an executive of one of the trade show partners. "That's not to say this organization wouldn't join the partnership in the future." In fact, representatives of the potential partner have attended the trade show, given it positive reviews, and stated that "the door wasn't completely closed" to future discussions.

Thoughtful Decision Making

The association involved in the Trade Show LLC spent more than a year evaluating the value proposition from both partners' perspectives. Association leaders decided to go ahead with the partnership after evaluating the answers to these specific questions:

- Would the partnership enhance our mission and provide more value to our core members?
- Are we doing this for the profit potential or to create a better educational environment for our members?
- Would this partnership diminish our brand in the marketplace if the trade show came to be viewed as the other partner's show?
- Would the additional audience delivered by the for-profit partner be able to expand our brand and our marketplace?
- How might the partnership affect our 501(c)(6) status?

In Different Leagues

Another factor to take into consideration is the size of the organization with which you might partner. If your organization is a "David," is it possible to partner successfully with "Goliath"—and vice versa? Based on the partnerships studied, both questions can be answered with a definitive "Yes."

Consider the profile of the Health Coalition, whose members include two large and two small organizations. From the outset, all four members decided that each would have an equal voice and share equally in the coalition's responsibilities and decision making. Each organization brings something different to the partnership, so its size is not a factor in the amount of value added. In this case, the two smaller organizations bring numbers to the general advocacy cause, enabling the coalition to speak for a broader spectrum of constituents and the public.

Pairings of small and large commonly occur in public policy advocacy coalitions. Often, they are also found in joint sponsorship/management of conferences. The smaller partner brings specialty expertise that enriches the conference program and diversifies attendance. In return, the smaller partner receives exposure to a much wider audience and larger facilities than it would have had on its own.

Quite simply, smaller organizations often have what larger organizations need—whether that's grassroots contacts, a unique product or service, a niche or diversified market, specialized expertise, an entrepreneurial bent, greater credibility, and so forth. For their part, however, smaller partners frequently have reservations about losing their identities when partnering with larger organizations. They may fear the larger entity, accustomed to wielding power, will overlook their desires or dismiss their concerns as not important. This is an understandable concern—one that larger organizations should recognize when initiating partnerships with smaller organizations. Additional questions and concerns commonly raised by a smaller organization include these:

- Will the larger organization even be interested in working with us?
- And, if they are interested, will our identity be swallowed up or lost?
- Do we risk losing our membership or our intellectual property rights?
- Is the larger organization's decision-making structure so politicized and/or convoluted that it takes an eternity to get decisions approved?

The larger organization in a potential partnership usually has one key question:

- Does this smaller organization really add value, or is this something we could do more easily ourselves?

Acknowledging these questions, which all have strategic implications, and being prepared to answer them might mean the difference between inking a partnership deal and walking away from an opportunity. For example, one 6,000-member association with extensive grassroots contacts received an invitation from a large media company to compete for the opportunity to form a charity-oriented partnership. Two board members joined association staff in making the creative pitch, emphasizing the organization's ability to deliver an audience at local levels.

In addition, says the association's executive director, "We were candid with the company, telling them that their selection of us would boost our members' credibility and help [our segment] advance to the next level. They were keenly interested in doing good things in local communities, and we had a network in place to do that."

Regardless of whether your organization is the David or the Goliath, you and your potential partner need to recognize the unique and valuable contributions the other brings. In this regard, partnership decisions should be consensual, without weight or regard to the relative size of the partners involved.

The Competitive Spirit

A partnership of competitors may sound like an oxymoron. Yet partnering with a rival organization that competes for the same customers, members, or market position is perhaps the epitome of strategic partnering.

Often, the motivation to partner comes from external sources, such as a shared threat or opportunity—usually in the area of public policy. Such partnerships usually come together with ease, because of the compelling nature of the issue. They tend to succeed for the same reason: All parties unify around the same goal.

More problematic are situations where the motivation to partner comes from internal sources, such as a board of directors. It's quite common for associations, especially those having overlapping memberships, to be directed by volunteer leadership to collaborate with one another on a particular project or initiative. The professional staffs, accustomed to fiercely competing in the marketplace, are usually reluctant to call a truce and initiate a partnership discussion with people they may distrust and even personally dislike. Nevertheless, such partnerships are not doomed to failure.

One such reluctant partnership between two professional societies that participated in the study started with a number of small, failed attempts to work together. Nothing much was accomplished—until both parties focused on a narrow task in which each could clearly see that it was in their interest to collaborate. Much like wary wrestlers circling each other, both organizations spent a great deal of time and effort defining the outcome each sought, then working out an agreement as to what each would contribute to ensure a successful venture.

In another partnership, the two competitors had a modest goal and succeeded enough to convince both parties to explore other areas of possible partnership. Step by step, over a decade, the two rivals came to regard one another with increasing appreciation and confidence. The competition cooled to the point where serious negotiations were launched to create a closer, more permanent bond between the two organizations.

Both examples illustrate the point that success cannot be forced at the board level, nor can it be achieved solely at the operational level. It requires board-staff teamwork to conceive and launch the initiative, a mutually recognized worthwhile task or joint process to be achieved, and careful planning and follow-through on the part of all involved. Forced collaboration almost always results in failure and frequently produces a greater sense of organizational distrust, morale problems among staff, and disgruntlement among members. But success in these cases, just like success in every form of partnership, can lead to accomplishments far greater than either party could achieve on its own.

How does one set up a partnership with a competitor? Very much like doing so with any other type of organization. Some additional factors, however, come into play. These relate mostly to the personalities of the leaders (both professional staff and volunteer) of each organization. If these leaders will be negotiating the relationship, all parties need to feel they can trust and be honest with the others.

When identifying the "right" rival to serve as your partner, look for

- Complementary mission and compatible goals
- Overlapping membership/stakeholders who can act as a communication bridge
- Complementary resources
- Willingness to engage in dialogue

Partnering with rivals is not for prima donnas. It takes a certain amount of humility to be willing to admit to one's constituents that maybe you cannot do it all, that partnering does make sense. So be willing to overcome a certain amount of skepticism—on your own part as well as that of your competitor's.

Participants in the virtual focus groups, for instance, reported a common concern about motive. They felt that rivals might have a hidden agenda for the partnership, one that might undercut their own organizations and do more harm than good. To overcome this, both organizations must proceed in good faith and lower their defenses when discussing the possibility of working together. Just as in every partnership, all parties need to believe that the end goal is not only worth the effort but also achievable only through the partnership.

WORDS OF ADVICE

"You can't do a partnership without open dialogue and candor. Politics and hidden agenda can't be involved."

– Senior corporate executive

Getting Serious

Every partnership, before it becomes "official," would benefit from a two-step confirmation process. Independently, each partner should do the following:

Ascertain the usefulness of the partnership for all parties. On behalf of your own organization, you've already answered, "What's in it for me?" Now answer the same question from the perspective of your potential partner. This step serves as a double check that the partnership would bring equal benefit to both your organization and your counterpart.

The partnerships studied for this book demonstrate that partnerships do not succeed when one partner clearly benefits more than the other, both in the short and long term. So, while your organization's interest may be clear and pressing, take the time to identify how what you have to offer will address your partner's strategic needs better than any other alternatives.

In the example of the Trade Show LLC, the publishing company outlined all of the areas where it could enhance the offerings of the nonprofit. After reviewing this information in view of its own needs, the nonprofit identified for the publishing company the area that offered greatest opportunity for a successful partnership. Eventually, the partnership grew to include other areas as well.

Acknowledge the cultural differences. Different organizations—and certainly different countries, if you are proposing an international partnership—have different cultural parameters. What's acceptable in one—whether it's the risk tolerance, the level of oversight, or the speed of decision making—may be completely befuddling to another.

One partnership, for example, found it difficult to accomplish anything because so many people in each organization needed to approve every decision. The solution was to appoint one person within each organization who was responsible for keeping track of the partnership and had decision-making authority. This streamlined the decision-making process of the partnership.

Because it was familiar with its potential partner's structure and approval processes, the publishing company involved in the Trade Show LLC had the patience to wait 18 months before the association agreed to the partnership. On the other side of the coin, one professional society closed a partnership deal with a corporation in just two hours. "Many of our members are entrepreneurs," explains a vice president of the association, "so when we see something that will work, we go with it."

Communicating in a Different Culture

"Our meetings were so positive—we actually had bought our plane tickets to attend the final session in Paris where we thought our agreement was going to be signed," recalled the executive of a U.S.-based nonprofit organization. "We called to confirm we were coming and were told there was no need. The agreement is off—and we don't even know why!"

The association executive's confusion probably stemmed from a classic case of cultural misunderstanding. It's something to consciously guard against, especially if you're planning to partner with an organization with its cultural roots outside the United States.

As products of a low-context culture, Americans typically say what they mean and do what they say—and they appreciate the same straightforwardness in others. Americans rarely have a problem working with total strangers; they assume that if the partners have the right agreement, with the right terms and conditions, everyone can shake hands on the deal and turn it over to the lawyers or staff to work out the details. It's even possible to finalize a deal in a single meeting. And, should anything go wrong, Americans will just bring the lawyers back in to straighten matters out. Then everyone moves on.

All English-speaking countries tend to be low context, while most other countries are high context. Most of continental Europe has a high-context culture, as does Japan. The Japanese are famous for smiling and saying "Hai" (Yes). But most American businesspeople have learned that this response doesn't necessarily mean their Japanese counterparts are in agreement. Rather, they're acknowledging that "Yes, I hear what you are saying."

Meetings in high-context cultures can be frustrating and puzzling affairs for an outsider from a low-context culture. Meetings outside of the United States often start with what Americans might consider "inappropriate" questions, such as "Are you married?" "How old are your children?" "Where does your family come from?"

In high-context cultures, such get-acquainted "small talk" has a purpose: to help executives evaluate whether to grant you, a stranger, access to their inner circle. The fact that you are having this first meeting means you have established some level of credibility. Whether you are invited back depends on how the executives gauge your trustworthiness, your seriousness about the business at hand, and your reliability as a partner for the long term.

continued on next page

continued from previous page

Now back to the case of the canceled meeting in Paris. There is, of course, more to the story. The first meeting went well indeed and led to a follow-up meeting. The Americans viewed the second meeting as the time to set the terms of the deal. Despite having to work through a French interpreter, they got down to business fast. In one day, they defined all the terms of the arrangements and then headed back to the airport. The third meeting, in the Americans' minds, was a formality—one in which a broader group of directors would bless the deal. But that third meeting never happened.

The Americans assumed they had the elements of a deal after the first meeting, and they undoubtedly did. But did they still have an agreement after the second meeting? They thought so. More likely, they completely missed the signals being sent in a high-context culture.

In high-context cultures, business deals are most often struck among friends, family relations, and other close associates. Quick deals are unheard of. More than likely the company's leaders have spent their professional lives developing this business, and they expect to spend what remains of their useful working lives continuing to build it. So, if you want their cooperation, you will have to deal with them on their terms, or you won't have their business—it's as simple as that.

Strangers usually do not succeed in this environment, and lawyers don't have much of a role to play in cultures where verbal agreements and understandings are often considered more serious and binding than written contracts. In truth, they are more binding because personal honor and integrity are at stake, and these qualities are valued more than money. Don't make the error of believing otherwise.

Talking Points

- What networking situations might present good opportunities to identify potential partners?
- Do we already know some organizations whose strategic needs might align with or complement our own?
- What can we bring to a partnership with a larger organization? With a smaller organization? With a rival?
- What is an appropriate time frame for the partnership we plan to pursue?
- What do we know about the organization's culture, credibility, resources, and acceptance of risk?
- What else do we want to know to prepare for a preliminary conversation about partnering?
- What questions about the other organization would we want to answer thoroughly before embarking on a partnership?

chapter four

Formation: Formalizing the Partnership

ONCE YOU'VE IDENTIFIED a partner, ensured that your strategic priorities complement one another, and mentally prepared to bridge any cultural divides, it's time for the third stage of partnering: Formation. Here's what you'll need to do next:

1. Define the goal for the partnership, and identify how each partner will offer tactical support to achieve the shared goal. This step may require some negotiations and many clarifications, such as which partner will handle an event's logistics, which one will collect the revenue, whether one partner has permission to use the other's logo for marketing purposes, and so forth.

As an example, the nonprofit organization involved in the Joint Educational Conference has responsibility for receiving and processing all of the conference registrations and paying all of the bills associated with the event. The government agency then reimburses the nonprofit organization for a certain amount of the shared expenses related to marketing and project coordination, among other activities.

2. Put the operational agreement in writing to guard against any misunderstandings. Having such a written document ensures that all parties know their tactical responsibilities and thus contributes to effective project management.

These operating agreements, while important, are often quite informal. The Joint Educational Conference partnership, for example, uses only one page to spell out the intentions of the nonprofit organization and the government department. The agreement notes that the parties will work out any disagreements in "the spirit of the gentleman's agreement which this is." The Health Coalition has been governed for more than a decade by a similarly phrased document.

3. Inform all stakeholders. This enables them to not only understand the reasons behind the partnership but also provide support.

As soon as they agreed in principle to jointly own the Trade Show LLC, the association and the for-profit company provided their boards of directors with formal notice of their intent to partner. Although the boards were aware of the organizations' initial discussions and ongoing negotiations, they became fully apprised of the partnership's strategy and plan of action only after staff and a small working group of volunteer members recommended moving forward. Several association board members who served on the negotiating team also served as conduits of information.

Both groups focused their communication on the big picture—the strategic goals of the partnership, rather than its logistics—so the boards were more likely to see the overall benefits and less likely to obsess on the details. At the same time it formally communicated with the board, the association also alerted staff members to the impending partnership and contacted its attorneys to begin formalizing the relationship with the for-profit company.

4. Finalize and sign any agreements (whether formal or informal) deemed necessary for delineating each partner's roles and responsibilities. Formal legal agreements will be needed to:

- **Serve as the contracting entity on task-specific projects**. When a partnership must make a financial commitment to third-party contractors—such as hotels, publishers, law firms, or other vendors—a contract guarantees payment for the products or services they provide. Vendors usually have their own purchasing contracts, but among themselves the partners need to have an agreement that spells out the binding commitments they are making. Such agreements address the issue of who pays what, when, and under what conditions. For example, do the partners pay equally or, as in the case of the Health Coalition, pay on a pro-rata basis according to their size?

- **Protect from potential conflicts with an organization's tax-exempt status**. The association partner in the Trade Show LLC had concerns that the Internal Revenue Service might negatively view its venture with a for-profit company to increase attendance (and profits!). The two partners created a separate legal entity (a Limited Liability Company)

Common Ingredients

From the research conducted for this book, these six points emerged as being important to the Formation stage of partnerships:

- Sound strategic reasons served as the foundation for the partnership.
- The partners complement one another in various ways.
- The association's negotiating team consisted of the top staff and volunteer leaders, with the close involvement of legal counsel.
- The partnership agreement, no matter what form it takes, has a one-year term and includes a provision for withdrawing from the partnership.
- The principles of equality and consensus govern the partnership: All parties have equal status and must agree on any decision made within the context of the partnership.
- All key stakeholders were informed via a timely, concise, compelling document that offered no chance for competing political interests or concerns to interfere.

in which the nonprofit holds the position of board chair. This new entity served as the contracting entity for the convention's vendors as well as the receptacle through which to collect and distribute revenue. Most important, this legal agreement helped shield the nonprofit from any real or perceived conflicts that might compromise its tax-exempt status.

- **Segregate funds and protect an association from perceived conflicts of interest within its own membership**. The larger corporate members of one major national trade association wanted the association to partner with another nonprofit group on a public policy advocacy issue—a move that proved unpopular with the association's smaller corporate members. In this case, a separate legal entity segregated this partnership action from the association's general policy direction and funds.

Unlike mergers or acquisitions—where legal teams take the lead and the managing directors sign off on the final deal as negotiated by their attorneys—partnerships are usually initiated by those responsible for the organizations' strategic direction with the legal experts providing backup.

In other words, legal considerations are subservient to the strategic benefits.

Each of the three partnerships profiled in this book (see Chapter 1) chose a different means of formalizing the relationship. The three types of legal agreements are listed below, from least structured to most structured. These examples do not imply, for example, that every partnership between a nonprofit organization and a government agency should be based on a handshake or informal agreement. Each case is particular to the partners' circumstances, but together they provide a sampling of the broad range of legal agreements you can use to structure a partnership.

The Gentleman's Agreement

By definition, a "gentleman's agreement" refers to an unwritten agreement guaranteed only by the participants' pledged word or secret understanding (*American Heritage Dictionary*).

Of the partnerships studied, the Joint Educational Conference involves the least amount of paperwork. Each year, the nonprofit organization and the state government agency re-draft and re-sign the same basic operational agreement, which spells out the purpose of their partnership as well as their mutual obligations. And each year the agreement concludes with the same language: "Any items unintentionally omitted in this agreement will be negotiated on the principles that this is a gentleman's agreement and not a legally drafted document." A lawyer might cringe, but this approach has served the partnership well over the years.

Additional paperwork crept into the partnership only when the state passed legislation regulating government contracts with outside private entities. This additional agreement is a two-page, standard government form that identifies the time frame as well as the maximum level of financial commitment expected of the government in this arrangement. The nonprofit chaffed at what it considered the needless formality of this additional document but signed it in the true spirit of partnership.

This comfort level has personal overtones. More than once during interviews for this study, each partner voiced its confidence in the other, making statements such as, "I know they would never do that..." or "I know they like to have things done this way..." This almost family-like familiarity with one another has outlasted personnel changes on both sides. In other words, the written agreements are backed by the partners' bedrock trust and their absolute confidence in the partnership's value.

Simple, Straightforward, and Effective

Reproduced below is a slightly modified version of the simple partnership agreement for the Joint Educational Conference, jointly produced by a non-profit organization and a government agency.

Dear [Organization 2]:

This partnership is a joint project between [Organization 1] and [Organization 2].

This letter, when signed by both parties, serves as a Letter of Agreement between [Org 1] and [Org 2] for payment of the partnership expenses:

- All bills will be paid by [Org 1].
- [Org 2] will reimburse [Org 1] to pay for the following:
  - Half of the project expenses—development, preparation and printing of materials, editing, and project coordination
  - Event staff of [Org 2] personnel
  - All press release expenses
  - X amount for other partnership expenses (mailings, etc.)
  - Other expenses as agreed upon
- [Org 1] will pay:
  - Half of the project expenses—development, preparation and printing of materials, editing, and project coordination
  - All other expenses
  - [Org 1] will be responsible (contract for) for receiving and processing fees, handling all administrative functions of the project
  - Other expenses as agreed upon
- Any items unintentionally omitted in this agreement will be negotiated on the principles that this is a gentleman's agreement and not a legally drafted document.

______________________________	______________
Signatory of Organization 1	Date
______________________________	______________
Signatory of Organization 2	Date

The Detailed Operating Agreement

The Health Coalition began with an operational agreement written more than a decade ago. Ever since, that agreement has served as the basis for the year-to-year renewal of the partnership.

The only other agreement all the partners have signed is with the lobbying firm they employ to spearhead their advocacy initiatives. This document specifies what the lobbying firm has been retained to do, as well as how and how much the lobbying firm is to be paid.

Between the two documents, the operating agreement is far more important; although the four partners have changed lobbying firms several times, they have not changed how their partnership operates. Each year the partners report to their respective governing boards of directors what the partnership has achieved and request further financial commitment for the coming year. Each year the executive directors of each partner organization conduct a strategic planning exercise during which they determine the partnership's strategic priorities for the coming year and evaluate the lobbying firm's performance.

Interestingly, this partnership lacks a monetary benefit. It has produced changes in health policies and generated funds for research, but none of the partners conducts the research. The return on investment of this partnership is measured not in monetary gains but in progress toward the organizations' strategic visions and fulfillment of their respective missions.

The New Legal Entity

Because the purpose of the Trade Show LLC partnership was to enhance attendance and profits—and because the partnership involved a for-profit publishing company—the trade association's attorneys recommended the formation of a separate legal entity to protect its tax-exempt status. As a result, this partnership required an extensive set of legally binding agreements.

The partners established a separate limited liability company (LLC), in which each owns a 50 percent stake. Profits are evenly split between the two. The agreement also establishes a governing board composed of three representatives from each organization. The nonprofit, however, always retains the board chair position. Also, its three representatives on the board, provided they all agree, can veto any "proposed action [that] would adversely affect tax-exempt status."

continued on page 49

Issues to Consider Before Signing an Agreement

After considering the relevant tax and intellectual property issues and choosing the appropriate legal structure for the partnership envisioned (See Appendix A), an organization's staff must delve into the specific details. No partnership agreement is complete without taking certain matters under consideration:

Due Diligence and Quality Control. Before entering into any partnership agreement, an organization should become familiar with its potential partner. Governing boards of associations are obligated to exercise due diligence on this front. An organization's staff should be prepared to check references and review key legal, financial, corporate, and insurance documents. Avoiding negligence in the selection process—and on an ongoing basis—is key to avoiding liability for the errors and omissions of a partner.

Confidentiality. While not essential, it often is prudent to enter into a confidentiality agreement with a potential partner *before* beginning negotiations over the partnership agreement. Such an agreement can help ensure that the organization will not be damaged or put at a competitive disadvantage by the disclosure or improper use of sensitive information or documents.

Intellectual Property. Engaging in a business venture with another entity almost always involves the use of one another's intellectual property and frequently results in the creation of new works. Each organization should include a license to its intellectual property that limits the other partner's use of that property solely to the purposes of the partnership. An organization must preserve the right to maintain quality control over any use of its trademarks, service marks, name, logos, or any other indicator of the source of a product or service. Both partners should address who will own any works created by the partnership—both while it exists and after it terminates—as well as the rights to share in revenue related to such works and the right to create derivative works based on such works.

Form of Partnership. Each form of partnership has its own liability and tax considerations. (See Appendix A for legal definitions of different forms of partnerships.) Be specific. For example, an agreement to enter into a joint venture should state so explicitly. An agreement that represents a limited, one-time arrangement should contain a clause stating that as the parties' intention.

continued on next page

Compliance with Tax-Exemption Requirements. Tax-exempt organizations have to abide by special tax rules to maintain their tax-exempt status. An association's tax-exempt status is preserved by continuously monitoring the amount of the resources devoted to a partnership that generates unrelated business income, as well as limiting the unrelated business income itself. The agreement should state that the tax-exempt entity, at the very least, maintains control over the tax-exempt purposes and activities of the partnership.

Performance Obligations and Performance Standards. A partnership agreement must be clear about the precise obligations of each partner and should err on the side of being too specific. Partners should be required to perform with high standards of quality, professionalism, and expertise, and the agreement should contemplate adverse consequences for a party that fails to satisfy these standards.

Timeline. Any time constraints should be stated in the agreement. The phrase "time is of the essence" may be used to prevent late performance.

Indemnification. Most partnership agreements contain an indemnification clause. The basic obligation is that if one partner's negligence or misconduct causes another partner to be sued by a third person, then the party at fault is responsible for any expenses resulting from the suit, including judgments, damages, settlements, and attorney's fees and court costs.

Antitrust Compliance. Any provision that fixes prices, limits competition, allows for the exchange of competitively sensitive information, attempts to set industry standards, restricts membership in an association, limits access to particular products or services, limits the production of particular products or services, or attempts to restrict who may do business with whom in an industry, likely is suspect to scrutiny under federal and state antitrust laws. Although such a provision is not necessarily illegal, exercise extreme care and prudence in this regard. If the agreement implicates any of these—or otherwise limits competition in any way—consult with legal counsel before proceeding.

Representations and Warrantees. Every party to a partnership agreement should be willing to make certain basic guarantees (often called representations and warranties)—to respect the rights of third parties, to follow all applicable laws and regulations, to sign the agreement only if actually authorized to do so, and to perform all obligations in good faith and fair dealing. Many partnership agreements also spell out particular consequences for breach of these guarantees.

continued on next page

Term, Termination, and Transition. All good partnership agreements contemplate an exit strategy at every stage of the enterprise. A solid agreement will spell out the initial term of the contract, whether and how the term will automatically renew, and when and how the agreement may be terminated. Unless the agreement specifies otherwise, the law generally will permit a partner to assign its rights and obligations under the partnership agreement to any third party, as well as to terminate the agreement at any time for any reason. To avoid costly disputes at the end of a relationship, decide, up front, which partners will take which assets with them when they leave the partnership—or, at the least, specify a process for making such determinations.

This list is by no means exclusive. All partnership agreements should be in writing and generally should be reviewed by legal counsel.

Source: Jeffrey S. Tenenbaum, Esq., Kristen E. Sitchler, Esq., Ann Thomas, Esq., and Aaron H. Hiller, Esq., Venable LLP law firm.

continued from page 46

The methodology behind the Trade Show LLC bears further examination because of its thoroughness in addressing a host of potentially complex issues. For starters, the association operates within an industry where the major players are all known to each other and where several organizations have significant overlap in membership. Association staff believed the industry would see the unique partnership as a major coup and did not want the negotiations to derail before they could be completed. To maintain a low profile, only a small group of senior volunteer and staff leaders participated in the negotiations. Both the association and the publishing company also signed a confidentiality agreement; this enabled them to exchange financial information vital to structuring the partnership without fear of any data leaking out, at any time, to the trade press or competing organizations.

Once the negotiations produced an agreement in principle, the association's executive committee prepared a memorandum to the governing board. The three-page document announced the decision; provided background information; and explained why the partnership was structured as a separate entity, why this particular partner made the most sense, how the partnership would be managed, and how the partnership would likely affect the association's operations. It concluded with an upbeat appraisal of what the association could expect as results. Three days later the LLC was established.

The document establishing the limited liability company addresses all the points required by the state in which the company is registered. These include 11 principal articles:

1. Organizational issues (such as the name of the company and the governing law of the agreement)
2. The "purpose" of the company, including "limitations on the authority of members"
3. Membership in the company, including initial members, ownership interests, management makeup, liability of members, and the ability of new members to join
4. Capital accounts (how the start-up capital will be accounted for and managed)
5. Management (how the management and officers of the company shall be determined, meetings run, and voting conducted)
6. Allocations and distributions of profits
7. Restrictions on transfer of rights or responsibilities
8. How the accounting, records and reporting shall be conducted
9. Dissolution, winding up, and withdrawal when members withdraw and/or the company is closed
10. Exculpation and indemnification, including the purchase of liability insurance
11. Dispute resolution that specifies the use of the arbitration services of the American Arbitration Association

The association's attorneys played a prominent role in structuring the Trade Show LLC partnership, primarily because of the tax-exempt concerns. Also, the presence of the association's attorneys leveled the playing field in a sense because the publishing company included attorneys on its negotiating team. Nevertheless, while both sides exercised careful due diligence, the overall tenor of the negotiations was characterized by trust and enthusiasm for the partnership being created.

Talking Points

- Who should represent our organization on the negotiating team? Is such a team even necessary?
- Will a simple document, such as a Memorandum of Understanding or a letter of agreement sufficiently address the needs of the partnership? Do we need something more complex?
- Does the operational agreement limit misunderstandings by specifying each partner's responsibilities, funding level, deadlines, and other contributions to the partnership?
- How will we share ownership of any products or intellectual property that results from the partnership, including revenues?
- Have we communicated the agreement to our stakeholders to ensure they understand and support the partnership?

chapter five

Maintenance: Managing the Relationship

SUCCESSFUL PARTNERSHIPS DON'T just happen; they require continual effort by all parties involved. So even if you've identified a strategic need for partnering and have already formed a partnership with the ideal counterpart organization, you still must navigate the fourth stage: Maintenance.

Only through diligent management of the ongoing relationship will a partnership prosper and thereby enable the organizations to achieve more together than they could accomplish on their own. What does such management entail? The research conducted for this book answers that question by pointing to six key elements of a successful partnership.

Six Key Elements

The six elements explored below were present in all of the partnerships studied. All of these elements are interdependent, overlapping and expanding on one another. Success in one area typically translates into success—or, at the least, progress—in another area. One the other hand, repeated failure in any one will cause the foundation of the partnership to develop cracks and eventually crumble.

While the organizations may not have consciously or deliberately recognized the importance of these elements in forming their partnerships, they identify the six elements as essential to ongoing success.

1. Mutual Trust and Respect

Imagine a sports team of any kind. All players share the same objective: to win the game. To contribute to a victory, each player has a position to play, and each position has an assigned role. All players know what is expected of them as individuals and as a team, and they trust their teammates to get the job done.

When all players perform as they should, the team succeeds; any player who fails to perform puts the whole team at a disadvantage. In this context, trust and respect are not luxuries; they are essential to enabling the individual players to work together as a team.

Similarly, a partnership without mutual trust and respect is not possible—not only because partners find one another through mutual compatibility of vision, mission, and goals but also because the partnership allows them to do together what they could not accomplish separately. Without trust, partners will constantly second-guess one another or question one another's motives, making it difficult to accomplish the common goal.

"There is a high degree of mutual trust in this relationship," says an executive of the publishing company involved in the Trade Show LLC. "We have respect for our partner, and we sense that our partner has it for us because of the open communication and the candor we've experienced."

In the partnerships researched, trust manifested itself in two ways:

- No partner makes a decision unilaterally without knowing the other partner is in agreement.
- No partner initiates an effort that will not benefit the other partner in equal measure.

Within the Health Coalition, for example, the partnering organizations do much of their work as a team. Each partner assumes the other partners will participate in conference calls, attend meetings, review documents, and complete other tasks that lead to group decision making. No one partner presumes to speak for the others—and the others trust such presumption will never occur. The four organizations also have a verbal agreement not to engage in individual advocacy activities that have the potential to dilute or compete with the coalition's activities.

The understanding that the participating members will always do what is best for the coalition came through in individual interviews. Representatives of the partnering organizations repeatedly used phrases such as "I know [our partners] wouldn't do that" and "We know that [organization] has the best interests of the coalition in mind."

The Joint Educational Conference provides an example of how trust and respect can overcome unexpected and severe strain. One year, an official within the government department thought it a good idea to solicit the participation of conference attendees in a lobbying exercise. This involved taking attendees away from the conference for a short time and busing them to the state capitol, where their presence would help draw attention to a gubernatorial public policy initiative pending before the legislature. The government official, however, hadn't adequately notified the department's partner of this intent.

This oversight nearly ended the partnership. The association's executive director believed this unilateral decision violated the basic spirit of the partnership and possibly placed some of the meeting attendees in a personally awkward situation. What's more, when planning the joint conference, the partners consciously agree to focus on education and steer clear of politics. Education sessions often discuss current or pending legislation, but always absent any particular political influence or perspective.

In no uncertain terms, the executive director communicated the association's unhappiness to the government agency. The association and the government agency then agreed that neither would ever take such unilateral action again. "The learning outcome of this particular instance was: 'No surprises,'" confirms a government official.

Both partners may laugh about the lobbying incident now, but they recognize that the misstep could have destroyed their strategic relationship had not deep, mutual respect been present. In this case, direct and honest communication saved the day and contributed to the partnership's continued viability. Rather than summarily cut ties with the government agency to make a statement, the association drew on the relationship's reservoir of trust and moved past the incident.

WORDS OF ADVICE

"Communicate everything. Discuss everything. If you are open about what you're doing and what's happening, the partnership will have fewer difficulties."

– Government official

2. Structured and Open Communication

Successful partnerships leave little, if anything, to chance. They not only formally articulate their strategies, priorities, and timelines for achieving their common goal but also establish a preferred means and style of communicating within the group.

Depending on the needs and nature of the partnership, weekly emails or monthly phone conferences may be the most efficient means of staying in touch and making decisions. One partnership regularly schedules in-person meetings so people can get to know one another better and therefore feel more comfortable in expressing themselves freely and frequently.

At a minimum, for example, the Health Coalition meets quarterly via conference call. Representatives from the four partnering organizations—but not the lobbying firm they jointly employ—participate in these calls. Outside of these scheduled calls, the members contact one another via email or phone call should any issues arise related to the coalition. The expectation is that each partner will "lay everything on the table," especially when a disagreement or problem arises. By openly discussing a matter together, the coalition can address and resolve potential problems in a timely fashion. Rather than getting sidetracked, its members can remain focused on what the coalition needs to achieve.

When building the upcoming year's advocacy agenda, the coalition's partners jointly review the previous year's initiatives and priorities and determine whether these remain relevant. They adjust the continuing agenda to address any changes or trends within the market or industry, then add any new initiatives deemed necessary. This all happens during an annual strategic retreat, during which the partners also review the lobbying firm's performance. No adaptations to the advocacy agenda or the lobbying firm's contract are made without a unanimous decision.

In general, as part of their communication efforts, the partnerships involved in the research

- Understand the need for regular, structured communication and incorporate this need into their strategic planning.
- Identify and employ the communication techniques and vehicles that best serve the partnership, not just satisfy one partner's preferences.
- Determine intermediate targets to meet within certain timeframes and financial budgets. This enables the partners to monitor performance against goal(s) and provide immediate feedback when unexpected obstacles appear.

- Create mechanisms by which to share feedback with the rest of the team and incorporate this intelligence into the overall effort. These mechanisms will help you determine how well the relationship itself is working, independent of the partnership's goals.
- Abide by an equitable and shared decision-making process (whether by majority, consensus, or unanimity).

Overcoming Common Obstacles

Partnerships have three built-in handicaps, all of which can be addressed through effective communication.

Obstacle: Each partner has its own regular business and operations to carry on. As a result, attending to the business of the partnership can easily become a lower priority or even an afterthought.

Solution: Write the roles and responsibilities regarding the partnership into the job descriptions of those who have a direct role in maintaining its health and success. All staff involved in supporting the partnership, for example, should be aware that their salary and job performance reviews take this relationship into account. If the partnership is not that important to an organization, it shouldn't be initiated or entered into. If it is important, each partner should be prepared to recognize and reward those who contribute to the partnership's success.

Obstacle: Each organization has its own culture, personalities, and preferred means of communicating. These differences often lead to confusion or stalemates in decision making.

Solution: Create a communication channel, select preferred communication vehicles, and designate one contact person in each organization as being responsible for managing the communication. This not only avoids bottlenecks in individual organizations but also establishes a separate communication culture for the partnership as a whole.

Obstacle: Different physical locations can limit the means and frequency of communication, leading to misunderstandings and delays in decision making.

Solution: Mandate regularly scheduled face-to-face meetings so representatives of each partnering organization can review results and discuss thoughts or concerns that might not otherwise surface in written communication.

WORDS OF ADVICE

"Communication has the ability to make or break a partnership. Don't rely on third-party feedback about your relationship with your partner."

– Executive director, professional society

3. Established Points of Contact

The partnerships studied for this book all maintained multi-level points of contact depending on the issue being discussed. In associations, the main contact is typically the CEO, with other staff members involved in day-to-day activities related to the partnership. For example, the CEO may negotiate the initial partnership arrangement and provide periodic updates to the governing board, while senior staff attend partnership planning meetings and handle communication with other partners. Staff members given responsibility for managing the partnership also have the authority to make decisions regarding the partnership without having to go through multiple layers of association decision makers.

Whatever the set-up, each partner's team knows who is responsible for what within one another's teams. This knowledge streamlines the working relationship by encouraging direct communication and eliminating bottlenecks. Problems are identified and addressed as they occur. The defined point of contact also allows organizations to more effectively measure the success of the partnership. At any time, someone within the organization knows where the partnership is falling short and how well it is reaching its goals and continually shares that status with the others involved.

One organization participating in the research recognized its partnership had stalled because its partner had not appointed anyone to follow through on action items. This realization prompted a reorganization of how the partnership was managed, including a requirement that each partner appoint a staff member to take charge of the partnership. Designating contact points enabled both partners to confirm that assigned tasks would be completed on schedule.

4. Complementary Vision, Mission, and Values

Vision, mission, and values are the strategic "glue" that holds a partnership together (see Chapter 2). When partners agree on these strategic elements, their joint endeavor will have a clear direction, a sense of purpose, and a targeted focus—and a greater likelihood of success.

This is not to say, however, that each partner must expect to gain the identical benefits from the partnership. The same outcome may deliver different yet equal benefits to each partner. In the Trade Show LLC, for example, the for-profit partner would like to see the show make money first and increase the value for participants second. On the other hand, the nonprofit would like to increase the value for participants first and make money second. Uniting the two organizations is their mission to make the trade show "the best in the industry" and provide essential networking opportunities for attendees.

The Health Coalition succeeds primarily because the four organizations collectively have mutual goals without direct competition. Although the partners compete for resources within the larger industry, they do not compete directly with one another. They find their common goal in the policy forum; the desire to reach this common goal keeps the organizations from pushing their individual agendas onto the coalition.

Additionally, the coalition has a consensus decision-making policy. In the end, a partner that may not completely support a decision will move forward with the others because it is in the partnership's best strategic interest to do so.

WORDS OF ADVICE

"Structure your activities around the goals and mission. Don't try to achieve too much that isn't possible."

– Senior vice president, professional society

5. Clearly Defined Roles and Responsibilities

Successful partnerships avoid the pitfall of thinking the other is responsible for doing something. They prevent embarrassment and frustration by establishing roles and responsibilities ahead of time.

- Which partner will be responsible for what and by when?
- Within each partner's operations, who has responsibility for which functions?

Most partnering organizations draft an agreement that outlines the desired outcomes, roles and responsibilities, expectations, measures of success, and resources contributed by each partner. It may be as simple as the one-page agreement used by the Joint Educational Conference (see Chapter 4). That agreement explains, for example, that one partner will pay all the bills related to the conference and the other partner will reimburse a certain percentage of those expenses, based on each one's available resources. In addition, a planning committee has been established to oversee the conference's details and meet on a regular schedule throughout the year.

The Health Coalition operates on the understanding that all four organizations equally share the decision making and staffing even though they contribute various amounts of financial resources. Each year, during their strategic planning session, the partners reassess the coalition's mission, goals, and objectives for the upcoming year's effort. The plan is fleshed out with the tactical details. Each organization knows what it needs to do and who must complete the specific collaborative task.

In the case of the Trade Show LLC, the contract between the two organizations outlines each one's responsibilities related to the corporate entity they created. The association, for example, provides staffing for the trade show, with the corporate entity providing the employees' compensation for their time spent working on the trade show. In addition, a nine-member show committee—with five representatives from the association and four from the for-profit—oversees the tactical aspects of organizing and operating the events.

6. Well-Defined Metrics of Success

Measurable goals provide a means by which to evaluate the partnership's progress toward its goals. A mutual agreement that outlines the resources put into the partnership and the desired outcomes provides a "report card" of sorts for gauging whether each organization is contributing to and benefiting from the partnership as expected.

Ultimately, a partnership's success depends on whether all partners believe they achieve more together than they would be able to achieve on their own. More tangible, specific metrics—determined at the outset of the partnership—enable each partner to make that determination. As the partnership

For Good Measure

To track and measure success, answer such questions as:

- What is the partnership's value proposition?
- Have we articulated the value proposition clearly, concisely, and compellingly?
- How will we know if the partnership is reaching its objective?
- What elements of value creation are most important to us, to our partners, and to all partners' stakeholders?
- What outcomes do we expect in terms of financial and market impact, organizational capability, innovative capacity, and competitive advantage?

Source: "Creating Successful Alliances," by Patricia Anslinger and Justin Jenk, *Journal of Business Strategy* (March 2004)

unfolds, these metrics should be revised and adjusted to accommodate growth and new opportunities that arise.

One professional society, for instance, used these three measures to gauge the success of its partnership with a nonprofit organization:

- Increased revenue for its members
- Increased attendance at its annual conference
- Increased media coverage of the conference and the society

Its nonprofit partner used one identical measure of success—increased media coverage—but developed additional metrics related to its strategic goals.

The for-profit publisher that participates in the Trade Show LLC sees the partnership as successful if it makes money and increases attendance. The association partner judges success in three areas:

- Growth in the number of exhibits and traffic at the show
- Satisfaction of attendees (How do they rate the show? What did they get out of attending?)
- Satisfaction of exhibitors (Did the show provide the right audience for their products and services?)

Although their measurements differ, both organizations agree on the overarching goal of having "the largest trade show in the marketplace."

In addition to developing measurements specific to individual partnerships, one trade association has three criteria by which it judges all partnerships in which it engages. This model evaluates a partnership based on its ability to deliver:

- A broader knowledge base and technical assistance to members
- Financial support to enhance members' institutions
- Advocacy for increased funding at the local, state, or national level

In all of the partnerships studied, the participating organizations evaluate effectiveness annually. None automatically renews the partnership without first comparing the partnership's performance to the metrics established at the outset.

The Role of Personalities

Whenever a key contact person or designated representative changes in a partnership, the possibility of other changes develops. Different personalities typically bring new dynamics and different preferences for communication styles, which can throw off a partnership's well-established balance. This isn't necessarily a negative—people new to a partnership may see vast opportunities where their predecessors saw only impossibilities.

During qualitative interviews undertaken as part of the research, participants were asked if personalities played any role in maintaining a successful partnership. All responded affirmatively, noting that their own partnerships would not work if any of the leaders maintained strict command and control over reporting relationships or insisted on doing everything themselves. Nor would their partnerships survive should any of the leaders act like prima donnas—people who want to receive all the credit themselves or prefer to be the focus of all publicity and media attention.

In other words, a partnership functions as a team. The team may have some "star players" with natural charisma or sheer talent, but those people devote their individual skills toward the pursuit of the group's goal. Above all, the players must trust that all of their teammates will always put the mission first; in a partnership, mission trumps personality. The research showed, for example, that certain personalities and friendships may help smooth the way toward forming a partnership, but sustaining one depends less on the people involved and more on the strategic goals.

Many partnerships outlast the leaders who originally started them. This fact proves that partnerships have strategic merit above and beyond the personalities who conceive them. It also points to the importance of putting in place teams and operational procedures that enable a partnership to survive changes in personnel.

Since the formation of the Joint Educational Conference partnership, the association's executive director has remained a constant. The government agency, on the other hand, has designated four different representatives during that same time. Despite these personnel changes, the partnership's mission and operational philosophy have not changed. And, even though some of its members have changed, the committee that plans the conference provides continuity as well.

In the way they divided responsibilities and structured the planning committee, the partners deliberately formed the partnership to prevent one organization or person from having a disproportionate effect on the conference. Early on, they established a culture of consensus and cooperation, with neither partner feeling the need to exert authority or demand complete control of the conference.

The Health Coalition, too, has survived despite staff changes at each of the four organizations. This is due, in part, to the ties interwoven among the organizations over the years—ties driven by self-interest as well as confidence built on more than a decade of frequent and candid communication. In addition, any change in staff leadership has been accompanied by a reaffirmation of the coalition's values and overall goal.

"Even if someone is not easy to deal with, the group always reaches consensus," says one nonprofit executive involved in the Health Coalition. "The group never lets personalities get in the way because the mission is too important."

Although the Trade Show LLC has not yet experienced any personnel changes, the partners have developed a culture that they believe will endure even as people come and go. As an executive of the for-profit partner says, "It's not so much a matter of personality as of the business mindset the person has." Both organizations have an entrepreneurial mindset and a strategic plan that emphasizes the importance of partnering, so any new staff would be well aware of the need to maintain a positive relationship.

Adding On

All of the partnerships studied for this book considered adding another partner or two, with some even initiating serious discussions with organizations having seemingly complementary visions, missions, values, and goals. None of these overtures, however, ultimately led to the expansion of the partnership.

At one time, for instance, several groups expressed interest in joining the Health Coalition. After many discussions, the coalition's leadership decided that expanding the coalition to accommodate the additional groups would dilute the partnership more than strengthen it. Instead, they advised these groups to form a network among themselves and pledged the coalition's public support of that effort. Still, the coalition has not ruled out adding new partners in the future.

"The coalition has a complex dynamic already, and another group could possibly complicate the communication," observes one of the nonprofit executives involved in the Health Coalition. "A large organization could possibly bring in more funding resources but has the downside of making it more difficult to stay on message and truly focus on the bigger picture."

"When choosing to add another partner, it's important to determine the benefit of adding that particular organization and whether it is as invested in your mission," adds another coalition partner. "What will that organization really bring to move the mission forward?"

The Tests of Time

Although they may have existed for a decade or more, the partnerships studied all operate with a one-year horizon. Each year, the organizations involved in the Health Coalition, the Trade Show LLC, and the Joint Educational Conference apply their individual metrics and conduct a candid appraisal of what the partnership has enabled them to do that they could not do on their own.

Having such a year-to-year or project-to-project focus provides all the parties an opportunity to take stock and determine whether they want to continue the partnership another year. Furthermore, such an approach allows "temporary" partnerships to adapt to a multitude of changes—including leadership changes—that may have occurred along the way.

Consider the Health Coalition, whose main objective is having a unified, strong voice on Capitol Hill. The coalition members need to work together to be viewed as likely to move forward. The organizations know that if differences between the members are visible they run the risk of losing their audience. And if the audience is lost, the overall goal of the coalition will be lost. Staff turnover within the partnering organizations has changed the personalities involved with the coalition, but the members' mutual respect has enabled them to adjust to these changes, keep the best interests of the coalition in mind, and continue to work together.

Partnerships evolve over time. Those that start out as task-focused may evolve into a process-oriented partnership as the partners grow accustomed to working with each other. When determining whether to enter into a partnership, one nonprofit organization even uses the litmus test of whether the relationship might offer the possibility for a merger in the long run. Mergers can certainly evolve from solid partnerships, although few start with that intent.

Most partnerships, however, follow the "sunset" provisions that exist in many government programs. That is, they identify a need and create a program to address that need—but make the provision that the funding is for limited duration, after which time the program automatically ceases. The expectation is that every program has one of three outcomes:

- Success but with new objectives identified that justify continuation of the program for another term
- Success, in which case the need for the program may no longer exist
- Failure, in which case cutting off funds is the right thing to do

The notion of limited duration imposes a healthy discipline on the partnership to achieve its intent within a budgeted timeframe. It also offers a graceful way to cut losses in failed relationships or to escape arrangements that have come to the end of their usefulness.

Talking Points

- What tasks are necessary to meet the goal of the partnership? Who will be responsible for completing each of these tasks?
- Have we designated a key contact person for the partnership? Has our partner?
- How frequently will we communicate? By what means?
- How often will we meet in person?
- Have we identified the processes by which we will monitor and assess the partnership's strategic and financial performance?
- Are we prepared for the unexpected? How would we handle an unforeseen opportunity or deal with a surprise threat to the partnership?
- How will we measure the success of the partnership? Is our partner using the same metrics?
- Should we consider adding another partner? If so, what criteria would apply?
- How often will we revisit the partnership to decide whether to continue or dissolve it?

chapter six

Exit Strategies: Failure *Is* an Option

A NATIONAL ASSOCIATION WHOSE members have direct access to youth markets once inked a partnership deal with an automobile company. Mindful of its members' sensitivity to any partnership that may have overtly promotional overtones, the association emphasized that the partners' joint efforts to improve youth-oriented activities could not "step over the line" toward blatant commercialism.

Within six months of the partnership's promising start, however, the automobile company wanted to modify the activities and always have one of its vehicles on display. "That type of promotional activity is not what the association or our members are here to do—so we cancelled the partnership," states the association's executive director.

In contrast, the same association has had a 30-year partnership with a large corporation to conduct competitions for youngsters locally and regionally; the winners go on to compete at the national level in the corporation's headquarters city. "[Our partner] really sees it as corporate giving in a sense, to really do something beneficial for kids," the executive director explains. "If the company were to turn the competition into a promotional event at every turn, our members would be turned off and it wouldn't be a successful partnership."

In the first example, the corporate partner's insistence on promoting its product violated the mutual trust necessary for maintaining a strong partnership (see Chapter 5). In addition, the automobile company did not respect the association's focus on its mission. On the other hand, the long-standing partner clearly understands that partnerships are driven by an organization's strategic needs.

WORDS OF ADVICE

"When the legal document is drafted, make sure it addresses what should take place if things go wrong. It should provide a roadmap for the partnership, including an exit plan if things fail."

– Senior executive, for-profit company

Staying on Point

Although partners may benefit in different ways—with some seeking monetary rewards while others seek primarily to advance their organization's mission—their joint success depends on maintaining a relationship that benefits each in equal measure relative to their strategic interests. A partnership that provides less value to one member relative to the value obtained by the other is "out of balance" and unlikely to endure.

Failure, however, is not necessarily a negative. For example, the association that initiated the end of its partnership with the automobile company did so to protect its mission and its members. Its strategic priorities took precedence over anything else.

Similarly, one of the foundations involved in the Health Coalition withdrew from another coalition because its partners exhibited more concern for their individual issues rather than the larger goal. Partners that bring underlying agendas to the relationship work first for their own benefit, which detracts from the partnership's strength and ability to succeed.

"That coalition tried to involve around 40 groups and had about 18 people on the steering committee," remembers the foundation's executive director. "With so many participating organizations and people, it was difficult to keep the big picture in mind. In the end, the coalition couldn't get the funding to make a specific impact on the larger mission."

The Health Coalition itself will fall apart when nothing remains to be gained that the four partners can't accomplish independently, says another executive director involved in the coalition. "The partnerships that fall apart

Proceed With Caution

Drawing on their own experiences and personal observations, respondents to the research's exploratory questionnaire identified the following as the top five reasons that partnerships do not succeed:

- Lack of commitment
- Hidden agendas/unequal partnerships
- Lack of agreement on goals in advance
- Leadership failure
- Mistrust/ego issues

either start out with partners that don't have much investment or things change over time and priorities shift," the executive adds. "Being in a relationship such as the coalition requires true dedication."

A Few Red Flags

Typically, attorneys become involved during the formation stage and when the partnership needs to protect against claims from third parties. But when one party starts using an attorney to gain an advantage over the other in an existing partnership, that is a clear sign that trouble is brewing.

Here are other "red flags" that can signal problems with a partnership.

Loss of authority or identity. This happens when one organization pushes its own agenda so strongly that it ignores or purposely overrides its partner's wishes, role, and identity in the partnership. It may manifest itself through misrepresentation of a partner's contribution, the promotion of a previously hidden agenda, or the withdrawal of support or commitment needed to sustain the partnership.

To minimize the possibility that the Trade Show LLC would be seen as "belonging" to one partner or the other, the two organizations created a separate legal entity to operate the show. This step enabled both partners to share ownership of the joint event intellectually as well as financially. They took this precaution at the outset of their relationship, to help avoid problems later on.

Some Lessons Learned

During negotiations with the publishing company with which it formed the Trade Show LLC, the international trade association noted key differences from its previous conversations with another potential partner. The partnership that never came to fruition had problems from the beginning, most of which related to trust—more specifically, the lack of it.

The trade association, for example, found its previous potential for-profit partner unwilling to share financial information; without such data, determining overhead and operating costs for a joint or co-located trade show became virtually impossible. On several occasions, the two organizations would seemingly agree to something; then the association would discover the other party had turned around and done the exact opposite of what had been decided.

Volunteer leaders, who were not actively involved in the partnership discussions, questioned if the association staff was creating too many obstacles. This placed more stress on staff members, who continued the negotiations in good faith but to no avail. Eventually, the association's board recognized that the problem wasn't with the staff but in the relationship between the two organizations.

"That particular for-profit did not have the same commitment to the partnership as we did and was very protective of its identity," says a senior director of the association. "Their mindset was always about the bottom line, about what was best for them, while the association focused on what was best for the attendees and exhibitors. We had to walk away."

From that failed attempt at partnership, however, the association sowed the seeds of success. The experience helped staff and volunteer leaders to clarify their vision of what partnerships could do for the organization and to assess their willingness to take risks in pursuit of future growth. When its current for-profit partner made an overture, the association came to the negotiating table with a wider perspective and a better sense of how to approach partnerships.

In forming the Trade Show LLC, for example, the association put a lot of stock in being honest and candid—and articulated the same expectations for the other party. The two signed a confidentiality agreement, which paved the way for their sharing of financial data without the worry of having that information fall into the hands of competitors. Also, the association negotiated this successful partnership with a team that included volunteers as well as staff, which generated greater buy-in and support among the board.

Consistently missing the partnership's goal. This might happen despite the best intent and goodwill of all partners. It's a sign that perhaps the partners' resources could be better spent somewhere else, either in identifying a more modest goal or in reconsidering whether the partnership itself was well conceived. Or, as was the case for one association that participated in the research, this situation may point to an initial underestimation of the amount of time and effort that staff must devote to making the partnership work.

Frequent breakdowns in communication. Partners should expect some miscommunication at the beginning of a partnership as they learn about and become accustomed to working with one another. But persistent communication problems can be draining, to say the least. Worse, they can lead to duplication of efforts or working at cross-purposes.

Ultimately, communication problems often lead to the partnership's unraveling. In fact, lack of adequate communication was near the top of the list when Vantage Partners, a consulting firm that specializes in business relationships, studied the leading reasons for failure. The other leading causes of partnership breakdowns were lack of trust, poorly handled conflict resolution, and an inability to work well with a different culture.

All of these issues stem from how people work together—and they can be minimized if, like the Health Coalition, the partnership has guidelines in place to assess and monitor its progress and a culture that accommodates new personalities. It's worth noting, however, that the Health Coalition made a conscious effort to become more cohesive and openly address "people issues" after a potential partner pointed out how much more the coalition could be accomplishing.

"End a partnership as objectively as possible—because you still have to live with each other. That is why contracts are so important; the emotion must be taken out if the partnership doesn't work."

– Executive director, trade association

Part of the Plan

Many organizations struggle with determining appropriate reconciliation and exit strategies, but doing so at the outset of a partnership is a good business practice rather than a portent of failure. Here are some options to consider:

- Include a cancellation clause in the written agreement. To avoid favoring one partner over another, the provisions should be the same no matter which party initiates the cancellation.
- If problems develop, have all parties agree to put the partnership on hold while they revisit the agreement and revise it to specifically outline the obligations of each partner.
- Have guidelines in place for communicating and discussing any changes that might affect the future of the partnership, such as organizational restructuring, changes in key personnel, new company ownership, or shifts in the legislative or regulatory environment.
- Develop a mechanism for annually reviewing the partnership before renewing it; this cycle provides a natural time to exit or end the partnership if it is not registering success.
- Hire a mediator, arbitrator, or another neutral third party to help work through any problems that have created animosity between partners.

Talking Points

- Have we noticed any "red flags" that might indicate our partnership is faltering?
- What provisions for ending or withdrawing from the partnership appear in our formal agreement?
- What lessons can we apply from any previous partnerships that either failed or did not perform to our expectations?

chapter seven

Primed for Partnership

As any of the people who participated in the research can attest, partnerships represent a lot of work. The best ones are approached strategically, with a view to how they can advance or enhance an organization's mission—whether that mission might be meeting members' needs, improving the public good, or expanding into potentially profitable markets.

Maintaining that strategic focus enables organizations to pinpoint the most appropriate partners and rise above the politics, personalities, and preferences that so easily can become obstacles between them. When strategy drives the partnership, the destination remains clear; the individual pressures and responsibilities associated with teaming up take a backseat to the ultimate benefits.

Is your organization primed for partnership? Before answering that question, take another look at the many considerations involved in working with another organization to accomplish something of significance that you are not currently in a position to do on your own.

Common Threads

The research behind *The Power of Partnership* did not uncover any significant differences in how organizations approach partnering. They all started with a willingness to take risks, financially and programmatically, and an openness to explore different ways of doing their work. In all cases, this meant mentally moving past what had happened or been done in the past to deliberately consider new opportunities.

Then, regardless of the industry sector or type of organization (for-profit or nonprofit, trade or professionally oriented), all successful partnerships followed the same four-stage approach:

- **Readiness:** Adopting a deliberate, proactive approach to partnering. This includes identifying a strategic need that the organization could not otherwise expect to fulfill on its own.
- **Identification:** Systematically identifying potential partners that would best fulfill the strategic need, based on complementary missions, visions, values, and goals.
- **Formation:** Thoughtfully developing the legal and operational structures by which the partnership will abide. These should recognize the end objectives of each partner, establish lines of communication and responsibility, set benchmarks and timelines for measuring progress and assessing success, and include an opt-out or termination provision once success has been achieved or the partnership fails to realize its potential.
- **Maintenance:** Providing ongoing support that demonstrates each partner's commitment to making the partnership work. This stage includes support from organizational leadership as evidenced by an appropriate amount of resources dedicated to the effort, to underscore the partnership's importance as a strategic priority.

Among those organizations that have had successful partnerships, two key findings emerged:

1. Each partner must benefit in some strategic way. In other words, the partnership must tangibly advance the strategic goals of each partner. Partnerships typically require too much time and material resources to be lightly entered into. For this reason, partnerships need to be able to show that they have made some tangible contribution to what matters most for each partner.

2. Each partner must understand and respect the other's needs. Although the partners' goals should be complementary and compatible, they are probably different—and those differences can create tension if not openly acknowledged. One-sided partnerships are an oxymoron, a contradiction in terms. A true partnership requires not only professional courtesy toward the other partners but also a demonstration of respect for their varying strategic needs.

WORDS OF ADVICE

"Revisit your agreement over time as your business models change. A partnership should be a collegial relationship that goes beyond the initial agreement."

– Senior vice president, professional society

Checklist for a Successful Partnership

Remember, partnerships combine the strengths of all the organizations involved to achieve a goal that would not otherwise be possible for them individually. Consequently, their mutual welfare hinges on the ability to foster teamwork and a sense of co-dependency. With that in mind, here are the basic steps needed for a successful partnership:

- Get prepared by having discussions with staff and board on how partnership can and should support your organization's strategic plan and mission.
- Know thyself. Identify the strategic need that your organization would have difficulty meeting on its own. Recognize what strengths, contacts, and resources your organization would bring to a partnership, as well as those it lacks.
- Do your homework on potential partners. Look for those that promise the "best fit" in terms of mission, vision, and values—not to mention the internal culture, including the potential partner's entrepreneurial mindset and willingness to share risks as well as rewards.
- Gather the tools needed to establish a partnership. Draft an operating agreement that outlines joint goals and objectives as well as the roles and responsibilities of various partners. What you learn about the other party during this negotiation phase may put an abrupt end to continuing discussions or pave the way toward a smooth, successful relationship.
- Finalize the partnership and its operating structure. Be sure to develop guidelines and "ground rules" for how the partners will communicate with one another, make decisions, protect one another's intellectual property rights, refer to the partnership in public, assess its progress, and resolve conflicts that arise.

- Designate one person to serve as the main communication contact or "manager" of the partnership within your organization. Ensure that the other party does the same.
- Periodically check the health of the ongoing relationship by assessing how well it demonstrates the six key elements of a successful partnership:
  - Mutual trust and respect
  - Structured and open communication
  - Established points of contact
  - Complementary vision, mission, and values
  - Clearly defined roles and responsibilities
  - Well-defined metrics of success

  Take action to improve those areas that aren't currently contributing to the ability of the partners to work well together in pursuit of their common goal.
- Have an exit strategy in place—preferably in the operating agreement—should attempts to fix a broken partnership not work. Know how you will dissolve the partnership once it has achieved its strategic mission.

As the research emphasized, partnerships are strongest when they are supported by a clear written structural outline, fortified by trust, and operated transparently with open and clear channels of communication at all levels of the organizations involved. In other words, a written document outlining procedures and accountabilities is a good start, but success ultimately depends upon the daily practices and attitudes of the people involved in making the partnership work. When they remain focused on a partnership's strategic merit, and how best to accomplish that goal, all of the parties involved will emerge as winners.

APPENDIX A

The Legal Aspects of Partnerships

By
Jeffrey S. Tenenbaum, Esq.,
Kristen E. Sitchler, Esq.,
Ann Thomas, Esq.,
and Aaron H. Hiller, Esq.,
Venable LLP, Washington, DC

The Power of Partnership uses the term "partnership" as most people would use the word when speaking to one another. When two or more people or groups pool their resources and collaborate to achieve a common purpose, it is fair and accurate to call them "partners." From a legal sense, however, the term "partnership" is a term of art—when lawyers describe two entities as "partners," they are speaking about a particular type of legal arrangement.

From a lawyer's perspective, a "partnership" is a complex interaction of business law, tax law, and the rules of intellectual property. Here is a general overview of the legal complexities that often come with forging partnerships, maintaining them, and amicably parting ways.

Basic Terminology

Strictly speaking, a partnership is an unincorporated business organization created by contract between two or more entities in order to carry out a common enterprise. Each partner contributes money, property, labor, or skill and expects to share in the profits and losses of the undertaking. Generally speaking, a partnership does not pay income taxes; instead, the individual partners report their share of the partnership's profits or losses on their individual tax returns.

Within this legal definition are several categories of partnership, each with its own balance of management rights and personal liability. There are also several forms of cooperation that fall short of the technical definition of partnership, but are nonetheless advantageous to organizations not yet ready to commit to a long-term relationship with another entity.

General Partnership. In a general partnership, each partner shares equal rights and responsibilities in connection with the management of the partnership, and any partner has the authority to bind the entire partnership to a legal obligation. Unlike shareholders in a corporation, the members of a general partnership are personally liable for all of the partnership's debts and obligations. Although often daunting, that amount of personal liability comes with a significant tax advantage: Partnership profits are not taxed to the business. Instead, profits pass through to the partners, who include the gains on their individual tax returns.

Limited Partnership. In a limited partnership, partners are divided into two classes—general partners and limited partners. The personal liability of a limited partner is limited to the amount he or she has actually invested in the partnership; as a trade-off, however, limited partners are not permitted to participate in management decisions. At least one partner in a limited partnership must be a general partner. General partners retain the right to control and manage the limited partnership but assume full personal liability for the partnership's debts and obligations.

Limited Liability Partnership. In a limited liability partnership (LLP), all partners may directly participate in the management of the partnership and are granted some protection from the partnership's liability—although the extent of that protection varies from state to state. Some states tax limited liability partnerships as corporations, although they are considered partnerships under federal law. Many states also make the LLP available only to certain professional businesses—for example, law and accounting firms—and mandate that LLPs adhere to specific filing requirements.

Limited Liability Company. A limited liability company (LLC) is a relatively new type of business structure created by state statute. Unlike general partnerships, which were developed over time by case law and require no formal documentation for creation, LLCs are created by filing a document (usually referred to as Articles of Organization) with the state. LLC owners (called "members") are not personally liable for the debts and obligations of the LLC. In most cases, an LLC will be taxed like a general partnership—that is, the LLC itself will not be taxed, and the individual members will report their share of profits and losses on their individual tax returns. An LLC may, however, elect to be taxed as a corporation.

Joint Venture. A joint venture is an enterprise jointly undertaken by two or more entities for the limited purpose of carrying out a single transaction or isolated project. Unlike a partnership agreement, which creates a new entity and anticipates a long-term and continuous relationship, a joint venture usually ends once its limited purpose has been achieved.

A joint venture can be structured like a general or limited partnership or an LLC, although LLCs are often preferred because of the additional liability protection and tax advantages. Similarly, joint ventures can be structured with an increasingly overlapping set of commitments between the parties and an eye toward eventually entering a more formal relationship. In any event, a well-structured joint venture will be codified in a written agreement that details the precise obligations and allocation of risk between the parties involved.

In a *whole joint venture,* one or more of the partnering entities contributes all of its assets to the enterprise. Trade associations, professional societies, and nonprofit organizations more commonly engage in *ancillary joint ventures*—essentially small-scale enterprises that do not become the primary purpose of the organizations involved. Organizations typically engage in ancillary joint ventures for a limited duration and memorialize the terms of their arrangement in a written agreement. For example, associations may enter into an arrangement with another organization to host a convention, publish a newsletter, or provide a series of educational programs.

Tax-exempt organizations seeking additional sources of revenue also may enter into ancillary joint ventures with for-profit corporations, as long as doing so furthers the tax-exempt organization's purposes and the tax-exempt organization retains ultimate control over the underlying activity. Associations often create new entities from which to undertake the joint venture. Depending upon the nature of the activity contemplated, such an organization may or may not be eligible for tax-exempt status.

Joint membership programs allow individuals to join two associations, typically for a reduced fee. These initiatives, which allow the members of one organization to become more familiar with another, are typically conducted in the context of other jointly run programs and activities. Again, programs in this vein are designed to bring associations closer together, often as a precursor to a more formal alliance, but allow the entities to tinker with the arrangement or disengage altogether if circumstances or expectations change.

Independent Contractor Relationships. An independent contract relationship is an agreement between two or more entities for the provision of goods or services under the terms specified in the agreement. For the most part, independent contractors are defined by the IRS's "facts and circumstances" test. For instance, if the association hiring the contractor has the right to control or direct the result of the work, but not the means of accomplishing the work, then this will be a factor in favor of characterizing the arrangement as an independent contractor relationship. Otherwise, the contractor may be treated as an employee of the association, whose earnings are subject to withholding for employment tax purposes. The employee also may be eligible for employee benefits from the association, among other significant implications.

Commercial Co-Venture. A commercial co-venture (sometimes referred to as a "charitable sales promotion") generally consists of an arrangement between a charitable organization and a for-profit entity that otherwise engages in a trade or business. In most cases, the for-profit entity agrees to promote the sale of a product or service and represents that part of the sales proceeds will benefit a charitable organization or charitable purpose. Commercial co-ventures generally resemble independent contractor relationships more than partnerships, LLCs, or joint ventures.

Because commercial co-ventures are relatively new, the body of law addressing them is still developing. Currently, 24 states expressly regulate commercial co-ventures. Although none of these states require the commercial co-venture to form a separate business entity, many do require that both the for-profit corporation and the charitable organization file a written contract with the state before engaging in any sales or charitable solicitations.

Protecting Intellectual Property within Partnerships

The various types of partnerships all likely will result in the creation of or involve the use of some form of intellectual property. Perhaps a company and a charity partner to promote a "green" program on each other's websites. Associations often come together to produce a convention or trade show. Several different types of organizations might enter into a partnership to create the definitive publication on best practices in a given industry.

Such business ventures likely involve the development of products or written works, advertising and marketing literature, the sharing of logos and organization names, and/or the use of membership and customer lists to market the program. In addition, business activities often require an organization to share its intellectual property—trademarks, trade secrets, and copyrights.

Trademarks. An organization's name and acronym may be trademarks protected by law. By definition, a trademark is any word, phrase, symbol, design, slogan, or tag line (or combination thereof) used by a company, individual, or association to identify the source of a product. A service mark is the same as a trademark except that it identifies the source of a service. A certification mark is a mark used by an authorized third party to indicate that their products or services meet the standards set by the owner of the mark. It is important to note, however, that several exceptions prevent a mark from being a protected trademark under the law, including the fact that the mark is too generic or is a merely descriptive term.

Trade Secrets. The term "trade secret" is generally defined as information used in a business that provides a competitive advantage to its owner and is maintained in secrecy. [See Restatement (First) of Torts § 757.] Almost any type of information, if truly valuable, not readily known in the industry, and properly protected, may constitute a trade secret. Trade secret information might include:

- Business information
- Customer or member lists and related confidential information
- Procedures, such as employee selection procedures, business methods, standards and specifications, inventory control, and rotation procedures
- Financial information
- Advertising and marketing information
- Processes and methods of manufacture
- Designs and specifications
- Computer software

Copyrights. While they often may not realize it, organizations regularly create and use copyrighted works. Under the federal Copyright Act, a copyright automatically vests in the author of a work as soon as the work is fixed in some tangible medium of expression. Essentially, when any entity puts pen to paper and an original work appears, a copyright exists. The copyright may be owned by a single author or by two or more contributors who are joint authors or co-authors. A "joint work" is one created by two or more authors who intend their contributions to be merged into a single work. As a matter of law, each co-author of a copyrighted work has an independent right to use and exploit the entire work but must share the profits equally and provide an accounting to the other co-author.

Organizations frequently miss a key copyright principle: the law treats works created by independent contractors and other non-employees differently than works created by an organization's employees. Materials created by an organization's employees generally are presumed to be the property of the organization, even absent a written copyright transfer or agreement, thus making the organization the owner of the copyright in such works.

However, even if an organization has conceived of the idea for a work, supervised its development, and funded its creation, an independent contractor (or any other non-employee) hired to create a work retains the copyright in that work unless he or she explicitly transfers it back to the organization by way of a written agreement. Even articles and graphics used and reused in the regular publications of an association may remain the intellectual property of their original creators and owners. If the organization wishes to continue to use such a work, it must obtain permission from the copyright owner and may be required to pay a licensing fee.

When such intellectual property assets are managed poorly, an organization runs the risk of damaging or diluting its rights in its own intellectual property assets and potentially infringing upon the rights of others. If managed properly, these assets can remain protected even as they are used to accomplish the goals of the business venture.

Preventive Measures

To protect and maximize an organization's intellectual property rights and avoid infringing upon the intellectual property rights of others, take the following preventive steps, either on an ongoing basis or when contemplating a new business venture:

- **Register copyrights.** Register the content on websites, publications, and all other important, original, creative works that are fixed in any print, electronic, audiovisual, or other tangible medium with the U.S. Copyright Office. Although such registration is not required to obtain and maintain a copyright in a work, it is a prerequisite to filing a lawsuit to enforce the rights in such works and it confers other valuable benefits. Copyright registration is generally a simple, inexpensive process that can be done without the assistance of legal counsel.
- **Register trademarks.** Organizations should register their name, logos, slogans, certification marks, and all other important marks with the U.S. Patent & Trademark Office. While federal registration of marks is not required to obtain and maintain trademark rights, it can be extremely helpful in enforcing and maintaining them. Trademark registration, although a bit more expensive than copyright registration, is still an affordable process—particularly when you consider that trademarks and service marks generally protect the actual identity of an organization or its brand(s).
- **Use copyright and trademark notices.** Use copyright notices (for example, "© 2008 ASAE & The Center for Association Leadership. All rights reserved.") on and in connection with all creative works published

by your organization. Use trademark notices on and in connection with all trademarks, service marks, and certification marks owned and used by your organization ("™" for non-registered marks and "®" for federally registered marks). While copyright and trademark notices are not required, their effective use can significantly enhance intellectual property rights, including putting others on notice as to their protection and preventing others from asserting the defense of "innocent infringement."

- **Verify ownership and permission to use all intellectual property.** An organization should ensure that it owns all intellectual property—or has appropriate permission to use all intellectual property belonging to third parties—that appears in its publications, on its website, and in any other media, and it should maintain and regularly update such permissions. Generally speaking, more copyright problems arise in this area than any other. If an organization discovers that it does not own intellectual property that it seeks to use as part of a partnership or business venture, it may be required to obtain permission from and pay a licensing fee to the owner of the work in order to make lawful use of the work.

- **Police use of your intellectual property.** Police the use of your copyrights and trademarks by others, and enforce your rights where necessary. Trademark law requires the owner of a trademark or service mark to take measures to enforce its rights in such trademarks or service marks. An organization may use periodic web searches, outside watch service vendors, or other means to do so. Enforcement does not necessarily involve the filing of a lawsuit.

Contractual Protections

Organizations entering into a business venture should memorialize their arrangement in a written contract. A written agreement will ensure that the ownership rights (or at least sufficient license rights) to all intellectual property created under the agreement are apportioned among the business partners as they intend. If an agreement does not spell out ownership of works, the default copyright laws will apply (see above).

Partnering organizations should be sure to address these areas in their written agreements:

- **Ensure confidentiality.** Potential business partners should enter into a written confidentiality agreement up-front—while they are ironing out the business terms—to protect the tentative deal, trade secrets, and any other intellectual or proprietary property revealed through the process of negotiations and due diligence investigations. Alternatively, the parties can address confidentiality in the comprehensive written contract that outlines their business venture.

- **Include an intellectual property license.** Any time an organization allows any other individual or entity—be they members, affiliated entities, or business partners—to use its trademark, service marks, name, logos, copyrighted works, other intellectual property, or proprietary information (such as names or addresses),it is licensing those rights to the other party. The terms and conditions of such a license should be in writing, and the writing should include certain provisions regarding the policing others' use of such intellectual property.

  The license of an organization's intellectual property to the other partner generally should be limited solely to the scope and purpose of the business venture contemplated under the agreement and should cease immediately upon termination. The owning partner should explicitly retain all key copyright, trademark, patent, and domain name rights created under the agreement; retain its ownership and control of the "look and feel" of any of its content used on a website; retain quality control over the use of any trademark, service mark, name, logo, or other indicator of source of any product or service; restrict the use of its name, logo and membership list; obtain confidentiality and security assurances regarding the use of its customer or membership data and other information; and obtain a warranty by the licensee partner that it will use no infringing or otherwise illegal material in connection with its use of the owning partner's intellectual property.

- **Minimize liability risk through representations and warranties.** An effective contract will include sufficient representations and warranties that each partner's intellectual property, software, website, and other elements that it brings to the venture do not infringe any intellectual property or other rights of third parties, do not violate any applicable laws and regulations, and that each partner will perform as promised.

- **Spell out rights upon termination.** While the parties may intend for their business venture to continue forever, even the best plans end or change. Thus, one of the most important issues to address in advance in the original written contract is what happens to each party's intellectual property assets upon termination. Joint authors who formerly shared all rights, expenses, and revenues, for example, may want to buy one another out upon termination or ensure that the other party cannot use or alter their joint work once they part ways. Partner organizations should consider whether derivative works can be created after termination, and if so, to what extent.

Before partnering, think ahead about what assets you expect to keep or to gain, what rights you wish to protect, and how to enforce those rights at and after termination. In certain cases, a written agreement may be required to alter the statutory default provisions that govern ownership rights related to these types of considerations.

- **Maintain agreements with contractors, authors, and speakers.** Partnering organizations also should maintain written contracts with any contractors and non-employee authors and speakers used under their business plan. If the ownership of works is not spelled out in a written agreement, the default copyright rule generally will apply. In other words, the person who creates the work owns it, regardless of who conceived of or paid for the work.

  An exception to that general rule is represented in the work-made-for-hire doctrine. If a work qualifies as a "work made for hire" under the law, the entity commissioning the work is considered its author and is the copyright owner, not the individual who created the work (17 U.S.C. § 201). This area of the law is complex, and many works may not qualify under the word-made-for-hire doctrine. Among other requirements, in order for a work to be considered a work-made-for-hire, a written agreement reflecting such status is necessary.

  A written agreement with any non-employees should contain a section that provides that (1) works created pursuant to the agreement are "works made for hire;" (2) to the extent a work is not a work-made-for-hire under the statute, the non-employee author, creator, or speaker assigns the copyright to the organization; and (3) in the event that the non-employee will not agree to assign its work to the organization, the non-employee grants the organization a broad, irrevocable, worldwide, royalty-free, and exclusive license to the work in any manner in the future.

Issues to Consider Before Signing an Agreement

After considering the relevant tax and intellectual property issues and choosing the appropriate legal structure for the partnership envisioned, an organization's staff must delve into the specific details. No partnership agreement is complete without taking certain matters under consideration:

Due Diligence and Quality Control. Before entering into any partnership agreement, an organization should become familiar with its potential partner. Governing boards of associations are obligated to exercise due diligence on this front. An organization's staff should be prepared to check references and review key legal, financial, corporate, and insurance documents. Avoiding negligence in the selection process—and on an ongoing basis—is key to avoiding liability for the errors and omissions of a partner.

Confidentiality. While not essential, it often is prudent to enter into a confidentiality agreement with a potential partner *before* beginning negotiations over the partnership agreement. Such an agreement can help ensure that the organization will not be damaged or put at a competitive disadvantage by the disclosure or improper use of sensitive information or documents.

Intellectual Property. Engaging in a business venture with another entity almost always involves the use of one another's intellectual property and frequently results in the creation of new works. Each organization should include a license to its intellectual property that limits the other partner's use of that property solely to the purposes of the partnership. An organization must preserve the right to maintain quality control over any use of its trademarks, service marks, name, logos, or any other indicator of the source of a product or service. Both partners should address who will own any works created by the partnership—both while it exists and after it terminates—as well as the rights to share in revenue related to such works and the right to create derivative works based on such works.

Form of Partnership. Each form of partnership has its own liability and tax considerations. (See pages 77-80 for legal definitions.) Be specific. For example, an agreement to enter into a joint venture should state so explicitly. An agreement that represents a limited, one-time arrangement should contain a clause stating that as the parties' intention.

Compliance with Tax-Exemption Requirements. Tax-exempt organizations have to abide by special tax rules to maintain their tax-exempt status. An association's tax-exempt status is preserved by continuously monitoring the amount of the resources devoted to a partnership that generates unrelated business income, as well as limiting the unrelated business income itself. The agreement should state that the tax-exempt entity, at the very least, maintains control over the tax-exempt purposes and activities of the partnership.

Performance Obligations and Performance Standards. A partnership agreement must be clear about the precise obligations of each partner and should err on the side of being too specific. Partners should be required to perform with high standards of quality, professionalism, and expertise, and the agreement should contemplate adverse consequences for a party that fails to satisfy these standards.

Timeline. Any time constraints should be stated in the agreement. The phrase "time is of the essence" may be used to prevent late performance.

Indemnification. Most partnership agreements contain an indemnification clause. The basic obligation is that if one partner's negligence or misconduct causes another partner to be sued by a third person, then the party at fault is responsible for any expenses resulting from the suit, including judgments, damages, settlements, and attorney's fees and court costs.

Antitrust Compliance. Any provision that fixes prices, limits competition, allows for the exchange of competitively sensitive information, attempts to set industry standards, restricts membership in an association, limits access to particular products or services, limits the production of particular products or services, or attempts to restrict who may do business with whom in an industry, likely is suspect to scrutiny under federal and state antitrust laws. Although such a provision is not necessarily illegal, exercise extreme care and prudence in this regard. If the agreement implicates any of these—or otherwise limits competition in any way—consult with legal counsel before proceeding.

Representations and Warrantees. Every party to a partnership agreement should be willing to make certain basic guarantees (often called representations and warranties)—to respect the rights of third parties, to follow all applicable laws and regulations, to sign the agreement only if actually authorized to do so, and to perform all obligations in good faith and fair dealing. Many partnership agreements also spell out particular consequences for breach of these guarantees.

Term, Termination, and Transition. All good partnership agreements contemplate an exit strategy at every stage of the enterprise. A solid agreement will spell out the initial term of the contract, whether and how the term will automatically renew, and when and how the agreement may be terminated. Unless the agreement specifies otherwise, the law generally will permit a partner to assign its rights and obligations under the partnership agreement to any third party, as well as to terminate the agreement at any time for any reason. To avoid costly disputes at the end of a relationship, decide, up front, which partners will take which assets with them when they leave the partnership—or, at the least, specify a process for making such determinations.

This list is by no means exclusive. All partnership agreements should be in writing and generally should be reviewed by legal counsel.

Tax Issues for Tax-Exempt Organizations

Before signing any partnership agreement, a tax-exempt organization should give special consideration to four central tax concepts. (Unless otherwise specified, the term "partnership" as used below refers to all forms of partnerships, LLCs, joint ventures, independent contractor relationships, and commercial co-ventures.)

Unrelated Business Income Tax

In general, tax-exempt organizations are exempt from federal taxes on income derived from activities that are substantially related to their exempt purpose. A tax-exempt organization may still be subject to unrelated business income tax (UBIT)—a federal income tax on income derived from a trade or business that is carried on regularly but not substantially related to the organization's exempt purposes. This tax is generally imposed at the federal corporate income tax rates.

For the purposes of determining UBIT, an activity is considered a "trade or business" when it is carried on to produce income from the sale of goods or performance of services. In determining whether an activity is "regularly carried on," the IRS examines the frequency and continuity with which the activity is conducted and the manner in which the activity is pursued. These factors will be compared with the same or similar business activity of non-exempt organizations. Discontinuous or periodic activities are generally not considered "regularly carried on" and generally do not result in UBIT.

An activity that is substantially related to an organization's tax-exempt purposes will not be subject to UBIT. In the context of trade and professional associations, an activity is "substantially related" if it is directed toward the improvement of its members' overall business conditions. Particular services performed to benefit individual members, although often helpful to their individual businesses, usually results in UBIT to the association where those services do not improve the business conditions of the industry overall.

UBIT is even a consideration when a partnership is formed by two otherwise tax-exempt organizations. To the extent that the activities of a partnership do not further the exempt purposes of either organization, income from the partnership may be subject to UBIT. Notably, if two tax-exempt entities form an LLC operated exclusively for exempt purposes and consisting solely of exempt members, the LLC itself may seek exemption under Section 501(c)(3) of the IRC. Accordingly, if the IRS recognizes such exemption, the income of the LLC would not be subject to tax. In contrast, the IRS will not grant general or limited partnerships exempt status, even if all of the partners thereof are exempt organizations.

An organization can jeopardize its tax-exempt status if the gross revenue, net income, and/or staff time devoted to unrelated business activities is "substantial" in relation to the organization's tax-exempt purposes. In an effort to prevent loss of exempt status, many tax-exempt organizations choose to create one or more taxable subsidiaries in which they may house unrelated business activities. Taxable subsidiaries are separate but affiliated organizations. A taxable subsidiary can enter into partnerships and involve itself in for-profit activities without risking the tax-exempt status of its parent. Moreover, the taxable subsidiary can remit the after-tax profits to its parent as tax-free dividends.

Control

In a partnership, a nonprofit organization continues to qualify for tax exemption only to the extent that its participation furthers its exempt purposes and the arrangement permits the organization to act exclusively in its own interests and in the furtherance of those exempt purposes. If a tax-exempt entity cedes "control" of partnership activities to a for-profit entity, the IRS will consider the partnership to serve private aims, not public interests.

In a partnership with a for-profit entity that involves all or substantially all of a tax-exempt organization's assets, the IRS generally requires the tax-exempt organization to retain majority control over the partnership—for example, a majority vote on the governing board. In a similar arrangement that involves only a portion of the tax-exempt organization's assets, the IRS has approved a structure in which the for-profit and tax-exempt organizations share most management responsibilities but leave the exempt organization in charge of the exempt aspects of the partnership. Even in a partnership consisting solely of tax-exempt organizations, the management of the partnership must remain with tax-exempt organizations and may not be delegated to for-profit entities.

Associations frequently enter into short-term partnerships with for-profit corporations in order to conduct a particular activity. These ventures should not jeopardize the association's tax-exempt status in most cases—even if the association does not maintain operational control over the venture—because the association will still carry on substantial tax-exempt activities.

Private Inurement and Private Benefit

In general, organizations recognized as tax exempt under Sections 501(c)(3) and 501(c)(6) of the IRC are prohibited from entering into a transaction that results in private inurement. Private inurement occurs when a transaction between a tax-exempt organization and an "insider"—someone with a close relationship with, or an ability to exert substantial influence over, the tax-exempt organization—results in a benefit to the insider that exceeds fair market value. Private inurement through dealings with tax-exempt organizations can carry individual penalties as well.

The IRS closely scrutinizes partnerships between tax-exempt organizations and taxable entities to determine whether the activities contravene the prohibitions on private inurement and on excess private benefit. The IRC also prohibits 501(c)(3) organizations from entering into transactions that result in more-than-incidental "private benefit" to another party, including unrelated third parties.

Charitable Solicitation Statutes

Over the last two decades, the vast majority of states and the District of Columbia have enacted and strengthened charitable solicitation statutes, designed to guard against fraudulent or misleading fundraising solicitations. The term "charitable solicitation" generally refers to requests for contributions to a tax-exempt organization or for a charitable purpose. Many state statutes restrict the application of their charitable solicitation statutes to organizations recognized as tax-exempt under Section 501(c)(3); others apply such statutes to all tax-exempt entities.

Solicitations may take many forms, including Internet and telephone appeals, special fundraising events, and direct-mail campaigns. Any partnership that engages in a charitable solicitation must adhere to the requirements in each state in which such solicitation occurs. While the specifics of these statutes vary by state, they generally require tax-exempt organizations to register before soliciting contributions from residents of the state. Registration typically involves providing general information about the tax-exempt organization.

Many states also impose reporting and disclosure requirements. Tax-exempt organizations are typically required to file a report or other financial information with the state on an annual basis. Many states make all or most of these reports and registrations available to the public. Some states also require solicitors to disclose certain information, such as the amount of the donation actually designated for charitable purposes, at the request of a prospective donor.

As commercial co-ventures have gained popularity, many states have enacted statutes that specifically address and regulate arrangements between non-profit and for-profit entities. Under these statutes, the for-profit partner may be subject to reporting and accounting requirements to both the tax-exempt organization and the state.

Alternatively, states may subject the partners of a commercial co-venture to the registration and bonding requirements usually reserved for professional fundraisers and solicitors. Failure to comply with charitable solicitation statutes may result in sanctions against the tax-exempt organization, including investigations, revocation of registrations, injunctions, and civil and criminal penalties.

APPENDIX B

Sample Agreements

Each agreement formalizing a partnership will be different, based on the strategic priorities, capabilities, cultures, and resources of the organizations involved. The first two examples on the following pages—provided by Venable LLP, a law firm headquartered in Washington, DC—offer ideas for the types of issues to consider when negotiating an agreement with a potential partner.

For additional examples, please refer to the *Association Law Handbook, 4th Edition,* by Jerald A. Jacobs (ASAE & The Center for Association Leadership, 2007).

CONFIDENTIALITY AGREEMENT

This Confidentiality Agreement (the "Agreement") is dated the ______ day of ________, 200__, and is by and between the ABC Association ("ABC") and the DEF Association ("DEF").

In connection with the consideration and negotiation of a potential agreement between ABC and DEF, ABC will, during the month of _________, 200__, be provided by DEF with copies of certain confidential information and documentation of DEF (collectively, "Confidential Information").

ABC covenants and agrees not to disclose or permit to be disclosed any Confidential Information, and that ABC will not appropriate, photocopy, reproduce, or in any fashion replicate any Confidential Information without the prior written consent of DEF. ABC agrees that any disclosure of Confidential Information in violation of this Agreement would cause immediate and substantial damage to DEF. ABC agrees to use all reasonable efforts to maintain the confidentiality of the Confidential Information and agrees not to use any Confidential Information for its own benefit or that of a third party unless authorized in advance in writing by DEF. Confidential Information shall not include information that enters the public domain through no fault of ABC or which ABC rightfully obtains from a third party without comparable restrictions on disclosure or use.

* * * * *

ABC ASSOCIATION

Signature: ________________________________

Name: ________________________________

Title: ________________________________

Address: ________________________________

Date: ________________________________

DEF ASSOCIATION

Signature: ________________________________

Name: ________________________________

Title: ________________________________

Address: ________________________________

Date: ________________________________

DC1/183073

AGREEMENT BETWEEN A NONPROFIT ASSOCIATION AND A FOR-PROFIT COMPANY

This Agreement, including, and subject to such additional terms and conditions contained in Appendix A hereto (the "Agreement"), is made as of this ___th day of ___________, by and between ABC Association ("ABC"), a ______________ nonprofit corporation, with its principal office located at __________________________________, and ____________________ ("Company"), a ___________ corporation, with its principal office located at __________________________________, and sets forth the terms and conditions of Company's relationship with ABC as follows:

1. Co-sponsorship. ABC and Company shall co-sponsor an event that shall be called "[Name of Event]" on the terms and conditions contained herein and in Appendix A hereto (the "Co-sponsorship"). The parties hereby agree to commit their best efforts to work together in good faith to carry out the Co-sponsorship and fulfill their corresponding obligations hereunder.

2. Mutual Web Links.

(a) Placement. In connection with the obligation of each party to establish a mutual Web link as set forth in Appendix A, the parties hereby agree to the placement of the Web links contemplated therein in order to mutually promote [Name of Event]. Each party agrees to incorporate the graphical image file provided by the other party into the HTML files located on its own Web site, subject to such image being of a reasonable size and form for the receiving party's Web site. The link shall appear on the relevant party's home page or such other page designated by the party requesting the link. Such link shall appear on the relevant page such that the user will see the entire graphical image associated with the link. Such link shall be subject to the terms and conditions herein.

(b) Content. The content on the pages containing the relevant links shall not be inconsistent with the parties' mutual intent to co-sponsor and promote [Name of Event].

3. Intellectual Property.

(a) Except as expressly provided herein, no property, license, permission, or interest of any kind in or to the use of any trademark, service mark, logo, acronym, trade name, color combination, insignia, or device owned or used by either party is or is intended to be given or transferred to or acquired by the other party by the execution, performance or nonperformance of this Agreement or any part thereof. Each party agrees that it shall in no way contest or deny the validity of, or the right or title of the other party in or to, such trademarks, service marks, logos, acronyms, trade names, color combinations, insignias, or devices, by reason of this Agreement, and shall not encourage or assist others directly or indirectly to do so, during the Term of this Agreement (as defined below) and thereafter. In addition, neither party shall utilize any such trademark, service mark, logo, acronym, trade name, color combination, insignia, or device of the other party in any manner that diminishes its value; discredits or tarnishes the reputation and goodwill of the other party; is false or misleading; violates the rights of others; violates any law, regulation or other public policy; or mischaracterizes the relationship between ABC and Company, including, but not limited to, and except as otherwise provided herein, any such use that might reasonably be construed as an endorsement, approval, sponsorship, or certification by the owner or user of such trademark, service mark, logo, acronym, trade name, color combination, insignia, or device of the other party or its services or products. Upon the termination or expiration of this Agreement, any and all rights or privileges of each party to the use of the other party's trademarks, service marks, logos, acronyms, trade names, color combinations, insignias, or devices shall cease. ABC and Company shall jointly and severally own the name and all rights to the mark "[Name of Event]." Upon the termination or expiration of this Agreement, ABC and Company shall each have the full, unencumbered right to use the mark "[Name of Event]."

(b) For the Term of this Agreement, both parties hereby grant to each other a limited, non-exclusive license to use, copy and display trademarks, service marks, logos, acronyms, advertisements, and promotional copy on or in their Web sites, promotional materials, and advertising and other marketing materials that promote the ABC International Conference and Exposition and/or [Name of Event].

4. Term and Termination. Subject to the terms herein, this Agreement shall remain in effect from the date and year first above written until the third anniversary of thereof, unless terminated earlier by either party as set forth herein. This Agreement shall not automatically renew upon the expiration of this three (3)-year term. Upon the termination or expiration of this Agreement, all rights to the mark "[Name of Event]" shall belong jointly and severally to each party, and the mark may be used thereafter by either party. ABC or Company may terminate this Agreement with or without cause by giving notice to the other party within sixty (60) days following the last day of any ABC International Conference and Exposition or [Name of Event].

5. Equipment and Materials, Expenses and Insurance. Each party shall pay all of its ordinary expenses arising from the performance of its obligations hereunder. Both parties shall carry general commercial liability in reasonable amounts, which in any event shall be in the amount of at least one million dollars. ABC shall not provide insurance coverage of any kind for Company and Company shall not provide insurance coverage of any kind to ABC.

6. Relationship. ABC and Company are equal co-sponsors of [Name of Event]. Each parties' directors, officers, employees, and other representatives shall have no authority to enter into any agreements or contracts on behalf of the other party, or to bind the other party in any way, and they shall not represent, either explicitly or implicitly, that they possesses any such authority. In connection with the organizing of [Name of Event], the parties may need to enter into agreements with third parties and make financial and other commitments. In such event, no party shall enter into any agreement or make any financial or other commitment in connection with the activities contemplated hereunder without the prior written approval of the other party. The parties agree that the parties shall share equally the costs and responsibility for such commitments. Each party shall be liable for fifty percent (50%) of such commitments, and shall pay such share directly to the third parties, or at ABC's option, prepay or reimburse ABC such amounts. After first paying each party for their reimbursable costs and other pre-approved costs and financial commitments, revenue from [Name of Event] shall be divided in equal shares between ABC and Company. Each party's directors, officers, employees, and other representatives are not, nor shall they be deemed to be for any purpose, employees or agents of the other party. Neither party shall be responsible to the other party or its directors, officers, employees, or other representatives, or to any governmental authority, for the payment or withholding of any federal, state or local income, unemployment or other employment-related taxes in connection with the performance of the other party's obligations hereunder. It is understood that neither party shall withhold from the other party's compensation any amount that would normally be withheld from an employee's pay and both parties warrant and agrees to pay all federal, state and local taxes incurred and chargeable to it in connection with the performance of their obligations hereunder. Both parties further warrant and agree to file all required forms and make all federal, state or local tax payments appropriate and necessary to the status of either party and its directors, officers, employees, and other representatives as an independent contractor and shall not claim any other status. Both parties further warrant and agree to file all other required forms, registrations, reports, and other filings, and to pay all corresponding fees or other charges, as may be required of either party, at the federal, state and/or local levels, as a consequence of activities contemplated hereunder.

7. Indemnification. Each party agree to indemnify, save and hold the other party harmless from and against any and all losses, expenses (including, but not limited to, payroll and income taxes and attorneys' fees), damages, claims, suits, demands, judgments, and causes of action of any nature arising from or as a result of (i) the performance of such party's obligations under this Agreement, (ii) the failure of such party or any of its directors, officers, employees, or other representatives to comply with any term or condition (including but not limited to all payment terms, warranties and representations) of this Agreement, (iii) the willful or negligent acts of such party or its employees, and/or (iv) the reclassification for employment or tax purposes of any director, officer, employee, or other representative of such party.

8. Conflict of Interest. Both parties represent and warrant that they have no business, professional, personal, or other interests, including but not limited to the representation of other clients that would conflict in any manner or degree with the performance of its obligations under this Agreement. If any such actual or potential conflict of interest arises during the Term of this Agreement, each shall immediately inform the other in writing of such conflict. If, in the reasonable judgment of the other party, such conflict poses a material conflict to and with the performance of obligations under this Agreement, then parties may terminate this Agreement immediately upon written notice; such termination of the Agreement shall be effective upon the receipt of such notice. Nothing herein shall preclude either party's directors, officers, employees, or other representatives from engaging in other business activities, so long as such other activities do not violate or are not inconsistent with the terms and conditions of this Agreement, or do not otherwise pose a conflict of interest with such party's obligations under this Agreement.

9. Nondisclosure of Confidential and Proprietary Information.

(a) As a result of the relationship created hereunder, either party and its directors, officers, employees, or other representatives may have access to confidential and proprietary information concerning the other party's organization, employees, members, and otherwise, including but not limited to, information concerning such other party's organization and structure, business, membership and marketing plans, financial data, the identity of past, present and prospective members, current and prospective contracts, and programs, activities, policies, standards, procedures, and practices (hereinafter referred to as "Confidential Information"). Each party acknowledges that the use of Confidential Information for the benefit of any person or entity and the disclosure of such information would cause severe competitive and financial damage to each party.

(b) Unless expressly authorized in writing, both during and after the Term of this Agreement, neither party nor its directors, officers, employees, or other representatives shall use Confidential Information of the other party for their own benefit or for the benefit of anyone else, or disclose such information to anyone outside of relationship contemplated hereunder. Each party shall use all reasonable efforts to keep information confidential.

(c) Upon the termination or expiration of the Agreement, or at any time upon the request of either party, the other party shall return all printed, audiovisual and electronic documents, data and other materials, including all originals, copies and extracts thereof, containing or referencing any Confidential Information or otherwise relating to such party's organization or operations, and all other property of the other party then in its possession or in the possession of its directors, officers, employees, or other representatives.

10. Miscellaneous.

(a) This Agreement contains the entire understanding between the parties and supersedes any prior written or oral agreements between them. This Agreement shall not be modified or waived except by written instrument signed by both parties.

(b) In the event that any part of this Agreement shall be declared void, unenforceable or invalid, the remaining parts shall continue to be valid and enforceable.

(c) This Agreement shall inure to the benefit of and be binding upon the parties and their respective executors, administrators, personal representatives, heirs, assigns, and successors in interest.

(d) This Agreement may not be assigned by either party, or the rights granted to or obligations imposed upon either party transferred or sublicensed by that party, without the express prior written consent of the other party.

(e) Either party's waiver of, or failure to exercise, any right provided for herein shall not be deemed a waiver of any further or future right under this Agreement.

(f) This Agreement may be executed in one (1) or more counterparts, each of which shall be deemed an original and all of which taken together shall constitute one (1) and the same instrument.

(g) Each party covenants, warrants and represents that it shall comply with all laws and regulations applicable to this Agreement, and that it shall exercise due care and act in good faith at all times in performance of its obligations under this Agreement.

(h) All notices and demands of any kind or nature which either party may be required or desire to serve upon the other in connection with this Agreement shall be in writing and may be served personally, by telecopier, by certified mail, or by overnight delivery (e.g., FedEx), with constructive receipt deemed to have occurred one (1) calendar day after the mailing, sending or transmitting of such notice, to the following addresses or telecopier numbers:

If to ABC: ABC Association

____

____

Attn: ____________________________________

Telecopier: (xxx) xxx-xxxx

If to Company: ____

____

____

Attn: ______________________________

Telecopier: (xxx) xxx-xxxx

(i) Each party acknowledges that this Agreement was made by the parties in the State of ____________ and shall be governed and enforced in accordance with the laws of the State of _________. Each party acknowledges that the state and federal courts of the State of _________ shall be the exclusive forums for the resolution of any disputes concerning this Agreement, the Cosponsorship, or [Name of Event], and each party agrees to submit to the jurisdiction of such courts.

(j) Both parties acknowledge that if either one of its directors, officers, employees, or other representatives breaches any provision of this Agreement, either party would be irreparably harmed, that monetary damages alone may not be sufficient to adequately protect either party from or compensate either party for such breach, and that, in addition to any other remedy, either party shall be entitled to recover all expenses incurred in enforcing these provisions, including but not limited to attorneys' fees and expenses, court costs, and to a preliminary and permanent injunction enjoining such breach.

(k) The individual executing this Agreement on behalf of each party hereby represents and warrants to the other party that he or she is duly authorized to bind that party to the terms and conditions of this Agreement.

(l) Both parties have read the foregoing Agreement in its entirety and voluntarily agree to each of its terms and conditions with full knowledge thereof.

* * * * *

IN WITNESS WHEREOF, the parties hereto have caused duplicate originals of this Agreement to be executed by their respective duly authorized representatives as of the date and year first above written.

COMPANY	**ABC Association**
By: ______________________	By: ______________________
Name: ____________________	Name: ____________________
Title: _____________________	Title: _____________________
Dated: ____________________	Dated: ____________________

DC1/114691

APPENDIX TO AGREEMENT

ABC Association will:

- Promote [Name of Event] via:
  - Direct mail (Event Guide)
  - Web site (including a link from ABC's Web site to Company's Web site)
  - Interactive Multimedia Webcast
- Provide advance registration services via ABC's customer service center and ABC's Web site.
- Provide onsite registration.
- Arrange for two meeting rooms at the [Hotel] on [Dates and Times] (rounds, head table, standing lectern, presenter microphone, overhead, LCD projector, screen)
- Perform logistical management
- Arrange for directional signage, podium signs and room identifier signage using [Name of Event] graphics logo.
- Provide attendee evaluation processing with post-event report to Company.
- Provide financial management: accept payment, process invoices, prepare reports, provide revenue share with documentation to Company within 45 days after the conclusion of [Name of Event].
- Provide tape and sell session tapes.

Company will:

- Identify and invite speakers for [Name of Event]. Provide speaker contact information and logistical requirements.
- Identify potential sponsors (see below)
- Promote [Name of Event] via:
  - The Company Web site, including a link to ABC's Web site.
  - Email newsletter
- Provide [name] as keynote speaker at ABC's Conference & Exposition
- Provide program description to ABC for promotional and logistical purposes.

Pricing for [Name of Event]:
Registration fees are $____ per person in advance, $____onsite.

Financial Agreement:
Revenue will be collected by ABC via the ABC conference registration process. ABC and Company will split net revenue less direct expenses (see attached budget). Company will be paid within 45 days of the close of the event.

Attachment (Budget)

MEMORANDUM OF UNDERSTANDING

This Memorandum of Understanding (MOU) summarizes the activities and responsibilities of [Organization 1] and [Organization 2], as these organizations enter into a partnership to support the specified initiative, and to understand and apply the outcomes. To solidify this partnership, both organizations agree to the following:

[Organization 1] Responsibilities:

- [Org 1] will work collaborative with [Org 2] to co-sponsor the partnership activities.
- [Org 1] will provide input on context of the partnership in development.
- [Org 1] will provide in-kind direct expenses estimated to exceed X amount for management of the partnership activities.
- [Org 1] will be responsible for the fiscal management of the partnership activities. It will provide [Org 2] with open access to all financial information to the partnership activities.
- [Org 1] will establish a process for communicating and informing [Org 2] on the progress and outcomes of the partnership activities on a regular basis.
- [Org 1] will insure the outcomes developed from the partnership activities are available and transferable to [Org 2].
- [Org 1] will identify the most appropriate distribution channels for communicating results.

[Organization 2] Responsibilities:

- [Org 2] will provide funding totaling X amount to support the partnership activities.
- [Org 2] will grant [Org 1] complete responsibility to work directly with the identified vendor to manage the partnership activities.
- [Org 2] will assign appropriate staff to serve as partnership liaisons.
- [Org 2] will cover staff and volunteer participation expenses for partnership activities and will provide direct and in-kind support for collaboration on meetings sponsored by [Org 2] that are not related to [Org 1] program of work.
- [Org 1] will review and approve the all final partnership activities before any established release to the public.

Joint Responsibilities:

- Products developed from the alliance will be jointly co-branded.

- The only logos to appear on the design of any of the final products will be those of the two organizations.
- Organizations' donors and sponsors will be acknowledged in aggregate.
- All press releases and other informational materials regarding the alliance and its outcome will only be issued after both parties agree to the language.
- Both organizations will maintain joint copyright ownership on all products, services, or tools developed as a result of the partnership.
- Both organizations will evaluate the partnership on an annual basis to review the process, strengthen lines of communication, and assess its effectiveness.
- Both organizations will equally share revenue received from the sale of products, services, and tools related to the outcomes of the partnership.

Confidential and Proprietary Information, Materials, and Property:

[Org 2] acknowledges that its employees and agents may be exposed to certain information, materials, and property related to [Org 1] and its activities that [Org 1] may consider to be confidential or proprietary, including but not limited to financial information, trade secrets, membership and other mailing lists, copyrights, logos, trademarks, and trade names. [Org 2] acknowledges and agrees that [Org 1] is the joint owner of all right, title, and interest to all information, materials, or property prepared, developed, used, or provided under this Agreement. [Org 2] acknowledges and agrees that [Org 1] is the sole owner of all right, title, and interest to all its own logo, trademarks, trade names, copyrighted information, and mailing lists. [Org 2] and its agents and employees agree not to use or disclose, or to cause to be used or disclosed, at any time during or after the effective term of this Agreement, any confidential or proprietary information, materials, or property of [Org 1], except as may be specifically authorized in writing by [Org 1]. Any and all such uses of [Org 1]'s confidential or proprietary information, materials, or property shall be subject to advance review and approval by [Org 1].

[Org 1] acknowledges that its employees and agents may be exposed to certain information, materials, and property related to [Org 2] and its activities that [Org 2] may consider to be confidential or proprietary, including but not limited to financial information, trade secrets, membership and other mailing lists, copyrights, logos, trademarks, and trade names. [Org 1] acknowledges and agrees that [Org 2] is the sole owner of all right, title, and interest to all its logo, trademarks, trade names, copyrighted information, and mailing lists. [Org 1] and its agents and employees agree not to use or disclose, or to cause to be used or disclosed, at any time during or after the effective term of this Agreement, any confidential or proprietary information, materials, or property of [Org 2], except as may be specifically authorized in writing by [Org 2]. Any and all such uses of [Org 2]'s confidential or proprietary information, materials, or property shall be subject to advance review and approval by [Org 2].

Effective Date and Term

This MOU shall be effective on the specified date, and the term shall be until the conclusion of the specified partnership activities. At the conclusion of the term, this MOU will be re-evaluated for subsequent participation.

Organization 1

______________________________	________________
Designated Signatory	Date

Organization 2

______________________________	________________
Designated Signatory	Date

References and Additional Resources

Anslinger, P. & Jenk, J. (2004). Creating successful alliances. *Journal of Business Strategy, 25* (2), 18.

Arsenault, J. (1998). *Forging nonprofit alliances: A comprehensive guide to enhancing your mission through joint ventures & partnerships, management service organizations, parent corporations, and mergers.* New York: John Wiley & Sons, Inc.

ASAE & The Center for Association Leadership (2006). *7 measures of success: What remarkable associations do that others don't.* Washington, DC: ASAE & The Center for Association Leadership.

Arya, B. (2007). Understanding collaboration outcomes from an extended resource-based view perspective: the roles of organizational characteristics, partner attributes, and network structures. *Journal of Management, 33* (5), 697-723.

Austin, J. E. (2000). *The collaboration challenge: How nonprofits and business succeed through business alliances.* San Francisco: Jossey-Bass.

Bartling, C. E. (1998). *Strategic alliances for nonprofit organizations.* Washington, DC: American Society of Association Executives.

Berger, I. E., Cunningham, P. H., & Drumwright, M. E. (2004). Social alliances: Company/nonprofit collaboration. *California Management Review, 47*(1), 58-90.

Boris, E. T. & Steuerle, C. E. (Eds). *Nonprofits and government: Collaboration and conflict.* Washington, DC: Urban Institute.

Cullinan, G., Roux, J. L., & Weddigen, R. (2004). When to walk away from a deal. *Harvard Business Review,* 96.

Dalberg Global Development Advisors. (July 5, 2007). Groundbreaking guide for businesses rates NGOs and UN agencies on partnership competence. *Corporate Social Responsibility Press Release, CSRwire.*

Dalton, J. & Dignam, M. (2007). *The decision to join.* Washington, DC: ASAE & The Center for Association Leadership.

Ertel, D. (2002). *Alliance management: A blueprint for success.* Boston, MA: Vantage Partners, LLC.

Gary, L. (2004, April). The growing reliance on alliance. *Harvard Management Update.*

Gazley, B. & Brudney, J. L. (2007). The purpose and perils of government-nonprofit partnership. *Nonprofit and Voluntary Sector Quarterly, 36* (3), 389-415.

Glover, S. (2001). Partnering for global growth. *Association Management.*

Gomes Casseres, M. (2005, August). Gaining benefits from non-profit/corporate partnerships. *Business and the environment,* 15-16.

Harrison, J. (2005). Why alliances are gaining momentum. *Mergers and Acquisitions, 40* (6), 28-31.

Hoskins, L. & Angelica, E. (2005). *Fieldstone alliance nonprofit guide to forming alliances: Working together to achieve mutual goals.* St. Paul, MN: Fieldstone Alliance.

Hughes, J. & Weiss, J. (2002). *Dealing with differences in alliance relationships: The three-layer Model.* Boston, MA: Vantage Partners, LLC.

Kliman, S. (2004). *Mending broken relationships: Foundations of success.* Boston, MA: Vantage Partners, LLC.

Kliman, S. & Parker Enlow, S. (2004). *A key partnering challenge: Managing both substance and relationship.* Boston, MA: Vantage Partners, LLC.

Kliman, S., Segil, L., & Visioni, L. J. (2004). *Implementing an alliance dependent strategy.* Boston, MA: Vantage Partners, LLC.

La Piana, D. & Hayes, M. (2003, November). A partnership continuum. *Association Management.*

Leigh, E. (2004, September). Cultivating corporate relationships. *Association Management.*

Liotus, B. (2007). The power of partnership. *Nonprofit World, 25* (3), 18-21.

Macdonald, M. F., Burroughs, M. M., Staley, R. S. & Stein, A. P. (2004). How do leaders of nonprofit partnerships foster collaboration? *Nonprofit World, 22* (3), 13-15.

Marks, M. L. & Mirvis, P. H. (1998). *Joining forces: Making one plus one equal three in mergers, acquisitions, and alliances.* San Francisco: Jossey-Bass.

McLaughlin, T. (1998). *Nonprofit mergers and alliances: A strategic planning guide.* New York: John Wiley & Sons, Inc.

McQueen, M. (2004). Us and them: Decoding the language of nonprofit-business partnerships. *Nonprofit World, 22*(1), 21-22.

Nichols, W. P. (2004). The prospects for radical change. *Association Management, 56* (8), 81.

Pietroburgo, J. & Wernet, S. P. (2007). *Investigation of association mergers.* Washington, DC: William E. Smith Institute for Association Research, The.

PR Week & Paine PR. (October 27, 2004) Survey reveals the nonprofit/cause-marketing forecast is bright: Nonprofits report ramp-up in corporate support and predict 17% increase for coming year. *Corporate Social Responsibility Press Release, CSRwire.*

Rigsbee, E. (2003). In bed with the enemy: How to partner with your competition. *Nonprofit World, 21*(3), 22.

Ritson, M. (2006). Sleeping with the enemy can pay off. *Haymarket Business Publications Ltd,* 22.

Shaw, M. M. (2003). Successful collaboration between the nonprofit and public sectors. *Nonprofit Management & Leadership, 14* (1), 107-120.

Society for Nonprofit Organizations. (2006). How to partner for success. *Nonprofit World, 24*(6), 12-14.

Strategic Alliances. ASAE's Essentials of the Profession Learning System. ASAE and Holmes Corporation. 2002.

Villano, S. (2005, October). Five ways to build productive partnerships. *Associations Now.*

Visioni, L. J. (2002, January). Preparing a successful partnership. *BtoB,* 9. (Vantage Partners, LLC).

Yaziji, M. (2004). Turning gadflies into allies. *Harvard Business Review,* 110-155.

About the Author

Plexus Consulting Group, LLC, headquartered in Washington, DC, is an international consulting firm that provides professional services to corporations and governmental and nongovernmental organizations. With affiliate offices in Beijing, Brussels, Geneva, London, Mexico City, Paris, Reykjavik, and Tokyo, Plexus Consulting Group offers services in these key areas: association management and coalition building, certification and accreditation, government relations; marketing, public affairs, strategic planning and organizational restructuring, member surveys, market research and statistics, conference and events planning, and information technology consulting.

Steven Worth, president of Plexus Consulting Group, has more than 30 years of experience as a professional consultant and has provided strategic consulting assistance to associations, businesses, and governments in areas covering organizational restructuring, public policy, and public and organizational communication. This includes designing and implementing strategies to create two world federations of nonprofit organizations, a global educational foundation, a national trade association and numerous trade and political coalitions. He also created the Association International Market Development (AIMD)—a program designed to open opportunities within USAID and World Bank projects in developing nations for the education, training, and standards development resources of U.S.-based associations.

Index